Books by Ruth Painter Randall

MARY LINCOLN

BIOGRAPHY OF A MARRIAGE

LINCOLN'S SONS

THE COURTSHIP OF
MR. LINCOLN

For Young People

LINCOLN'S ANIMAL FRIENDS

I MARY

" I Mary take thee Abraham to my wedded Husband . . ."

Mary at Nineteen

This painting of Mary fits the description of her by a schoolmate, "a merry, companionable girl with a smile for everybody." This portrait is by her niece, Katherine Helm.

I Mary

❖

A BIOGRAPHY
OF THE GIRL WHO MARRIED
ABRAHAM LINCOLN

by
Ruth Painter Randall

Little, Brown & Company

BOSTON   TORONTO

LIBRARY OF CONGRESS CATALOG CARD NO. 59–7358

FIRST EDITION

Published simultaneously in Canada
by Little, Brown & Company (Canada) Limited

PRINTED IN THE UNITED STATES OF AMERICA

To

all the members of my family
with whom I once gathered round
the long dining table
at the old home in Virginia

Acknowledgments

I WISH first to express my appreciation to Mrs. Thelma R. King, Director of Steele Memorial Library, Elmira, New York, for urging me to write this life of Mrs. Abraham Lincoln for young readers. After the publication of my *Mary Lincoln: Biography of a Marriage*, several people mentioned the desirability of such a book, and Mrs. King wrote me a thoughtful letter giving her reasons. She had reviewed my three books on the Lincolns for a group of young matrons who became disturbed because they had absorbed false notions about Mrs. Lincoln from older Lincoln volumes. One of them, wrote Mrs. King, said in effect, "We all form our imperfect ideas about Mary Lincoln in our schooldays. Why doesn't Mrs. Randall write her story for older girls?" I found this argument very appealing and shortly thereafter started work on this book.

It is a great help to any author to have a patient friend on whom to "try out" a manuscript. It goes without saying that you carefully select one in whose judgment and literary understanding you have full confidence. It was my privilege to read the manuscript of this book, chapter

Acknowledgments

by chapter, to Alice Harnish, who proved the most satisfactory and delightful of touchstones. I deeply appreciate the help and encouragement she gave me.

Another long-time friend has given her valuable assistance. Helen Hart Metz has again shown her skill and interest by making the index of this book.

I am indebted to Mr. William H. Townsend of Lexington, Kentucky, for his kind permission to use photographs of three paintings owned by him: the portrait of Mary Todd and that of her father Robert S. Todd, and a miniature of her stepmother.

I also wish to thank Miss Jane Merchant and the Washington *Star* for permission to reprint her poem "Valentine for Mary Lincoln." Miss Merchant's letter replying to mine about the poem completed a pleasing circle: she wrote me she was moved to write the poem after reading my *Mary Lincoln: Biography of a Marriage*. Since *I Mary* is based upon this larger work, all those who aided me in the years when I was writing it deserve renewed thanks here.

RUTH PAINTER RANDALL

Contents

Contents

I Mary

Hampering Opinions
of a Stepmother

*T*HE girl was tiptoeing down the stairs. Her eyes were bright with excitement and a kind of triumph. But she looked very anxious. Her steps were hurried and she was watching the doorways into the front hall in a way that showed plainly she was afraid of being caught.

The girl's name was Mary Ann Todd. She was about ten years old and had a round, pretty face with bright coloring. Her eyes were blue, her hair was a warm light brown, and her skin was unusually white. Just at this moment her cheeks were very pink, as she flushed when she was excited.

Mary wore a simple muslin dress that morning — her Sunday best — made in the style of little girls' dresses more than a century ago. But there was something very peculiar about this dress. Surely it was not ever the fashion for little girls' dresses to look as funny as that! The skirt of it bulged out in front and behind in two odd-looking curves, while it fell in flat at the sides in the most awkward way imaginable. Anyone could see that little skirt was not meant to be bulged out like that — it was bursting at the seams.

But to Mary it was a great success. She and her cousin Elizabeth Humphreys had worked very late in their room the night before to achieve those peculiar curves. It was the style at that time for grown ladies to wear fascinating hoop skirts that swayed and billowed as they walked and the two little girls had passionately wanted hoop skirts too. They knew very well it was no use to ask Mrs. Todd, Mary's stepmother, for hoops. Mrs. Todd believed, as many people did then, that children should be kept in the background and never do anything to call attention to themselves. It was not an interesting role to which little girls were assigned in those days. It consisted largely in being prim and proper and in doing what they were told to do without question or having any ideas of their own. The role did not suit Mary's lively temperament.

She and Elizabeth had had to do a great deal of secret planning before that Sunday morning when she started down the stairs. How could they make themselves some hoop skirts? What would they use for hoops? It was Mary who had the idea about the weeping willow tree. Willow branches were long and thin and would curve nicely — they would sew some willow switches into their dresses and wear them to Sunday school. What a satisfying moment it would be when they entered the church and people saw those fashionable hoop skirts and realized that those little girls were growing up into young ladies!

Mary had collected the willow shoots on Saturday afternoon and hidden them in the room at the Todd home where she and Elizabeth slept together. That night, after they were supposed to be in bed and asleep, they lighted their candle again and, taking care not to make any noise, they began work. It was not as easy as they had thought it would be because the willow branches were much thicker and heavier at the cut ends than they were at the tips. But at last they finished sewing them in the dresses.

Next morning after breakfast the girls flew to their room to dress for Sunday school. Mary, always quick in her movements, was ready first and started down the stairs. If only she could reach the street before her stepmother saw her!

Her foot touched the bottom step. Across the hall and out the front door she went like a flash. Why, oh why, was Elizabeth so slow! She was only now coming down the stairs. Oh, oh, Mrs. Todd was coming into the hall! Mary heard her stepmother call her name in ominous tones and knew their beautiful plan was ruined.

She came slowly back through the front door. She and Elizabeth stood guiltily before the lady of the house. Mrs. Todd, dressed in a lovely hoop skirt that swayed gracefully in a perfect circle above her feet, looked at the two funny little girls in their distorted dresses and laughed.

"What frights you are. Take those awful things off, dress yourselves properly and go to Sunday school."

The crestfallen girls obeyed. Mary, stung by that laugh, hurt, and quick-tempered, burst into angry tears. She told Elizabeth passionately that it was not fair. If only her stepmother had shown a little sympathy about her longing for a hoop skirt! When Mary wanted anything she wanted it with her whole heart. Perhaps her own mother would have understood her longing and have sympathized with it, explaining that she should have lovely hoop skirts when she was a little older but it was too soon now. Her stepmother had made fun of her and laughed. Mary poured out her wounded feelings to Elizabeth in a torrent of words. Elizabeth too felt unfairly treated, but Mrs. Todd was her own aunt, so she said little. Elizabeth knew how to hold her tongue much better than Mary did.

What made Mary feel more strongly about the incident was a fixed idea in her mind. She felt that it was not fair that she had this stepmother. Her own mother had died when she was going on seven. She was a very affectionate child and she could not forget the strangeness and awful feeling she had had at that time.

After that her father's sister came to keep house for him and his six children. It also helped a great deal that right next door to them, in the big brick house just across a strip of lawn, lived Grandmother Parker, Mary's mother's mother. With these grown-up relatives and two brothers and three sisters, Mary had a big family around her and was soon a cheerful, well-cared-for little girl again.

Then her father took for his second wife a pretty, attractive young lady named Betsy Humphreys. Grandmother Parker had been violently opposed to this marriage and had done everything she could to prevent it. Mary now for two years had had a stepmother of whom Grandmother Parker was constantly disapproving. It is not hard to guess where the little girl got her idea that having this stepmother was a grievance.

The second Mrs. Todd was a good woman, but she thought children should be brought up with very strict rules. She would often say it took seven generations to make a lady. It doubtless seemed frequently to Mary that doing anything which was fun or interesting was "unladylike" in the eyes of her conventional stepmother.

Mary resented this strictness. She did not like taking orders, though she would do anything for one she loved. There was an undercurrent of conflict between her and her stepmother which sometimes had the effect of making her feel insecure and unhappy.

Mary and Elizabeth were not allowed to forget the hoop skirt incident. The other Todd children, as in all big families, loved to tease and they considered the matter a great joke. The boys delighted in bringing in willow branches and presenting them to Mary and Elizabeth with great ceremony. They would suggest insultingly that as far as the girls were concerned, willow

Mary's Father and Stepmother

Mary thought her father, Robert S. Todd, the handsomest and best-mannered man in Lexington, Kentucky. But her stepmother had so many children of her own that she did not want her stepchildren, and this made Mary feel "desolate."

switches might have better uses than substituting for hoops!

Not long after that humiliating Sunday, however, the two received a thrill that just about made up for it. Mr. Todd had gone on the long trip from Kentucky to New Orleans. When he came back he had presents for them. Excitedly they unwrapped some lovely sheer embroidered pink muslin, enough to make each of them a dress. Mary was almost beside herself with delight. She knew just how she wanted those dresses made, if only her stepmother would let her plan them. This time Mrs. Todd let Mary carry out her ideas, and the little girl happily directed the sewing woman who made the frocks for her and Elizabeth. All her life Mary would love pretty, stylish clothes.

One day in the future people would talk about the taste and beauty of Mary's costumes. They would stare at her rich hoop-skirted gowns of satin or velvet as she stood in line receiving great crowds at receptions in the White House. That would be when she was Mrs. Abraham Lincoln, wife of President Lincoln.

• 2 •

A Big Family
in an Old
Kentucky Home

THE house in which Mary had been born in 1818 stood on Short Street in Lexington, a beautiful little town in Kentucky. It was a stately house with a fan-shaped window above the front door. Little Mary, as she learned to walk and notice things, was surrounded by rich furnishings, handsome dark chairs and sofas and lovely colored draperies at the windows. If someone held her up, she could see her eager little-girl face reflected in gold-framed mirrors. She caught the gleam of fine silver on the big sideboard. She would grow up loving all these things that make a beautiful home.

Her father, Robert Smith Todd, was a prominent businessman in the town and could well afford a fine home. He was a tall, handsome gentleman with brown hair and eyes and a ruddy complexion. He had married Mary's mother, Eliza Parker, in that same brick house next door where Grandmother Parker still lived. Both of Mary's parents belonged to what were called "best families" in Kentucky and both could have named distinguished and honored men among their ancestors.

Mr. Todd had Negro slaves for his house servants. The day Mary was born, it was probably the gentle brown hands of a Negro Mammy which bathed and dressed the newborn baby for the first time. As the baby grew into more and more awareness of the people around her, she found Mammy a very important person in her life.

It was Mammy who taught her what well-brought-up little girls should do and not do. Mammy was very particular about her "chil'en's" raising. It was on Mammy's ample lap that she sat to listen to strange, fascinating tales which were sometimes rather shivery. It was on that same comforting lap she was soothed and petted when she had fallen and skinned her knee or otherwise hurt herself. It may well have been to Mammy Sally's sheltering arms she turned blindly when, in her seventh year, she was told that her mother was dead. There was good reason why Mary all her life would love the Negro people and treat them with special kindness and sympathy.

By the time Mary was eight her stepmother had come to take charge of the household, which had four other servants in addition to Mammy Sally. Perhaps the most impressive of these was dignified old Nelson, who served as both coachman and butler, for his uniform included a blue swallowtail coat adorned with big brass buttons.

It took five servants to take care of such a big family. The new Mrs. Todd had six stepchildren to start with and in time she was to have nine children of her own. Under the circumstances she hardly had time to listen to or indulge Mary's impulsive ideas. Nor could she be blamed if she at times felt that six high-spirited, headstrong stepchildren were not exactly what she needed — or wanted!

In such a generous-sized household one more child made very little difference. Shortly after the stepmother came, she brought her niece, Elizabeth Humphreys, to live with them and go to school with Mary. This was fortunate, for it was Elizabeth who years later wrote a full account of their girlhood days, so that the details were not lost.

The two friendly little girls became completely devoted to each other. Elizabeth seems to have admired Mary in the way a quiet, rule-abiding girl enjoys one who is lively and daring. She found Mary good company and very affectionate. It did not take Elizabeth long to discover that Mary's tongue could be quick and sharp. Yet the only time she saw Mary really angry in the years they spent together was when her stepmother had laughed at their ridiculous attempt at hoop skirts and had sent them upstairs to "take those awful things off."

The two shared a room and slept together, doubtless in a big high bed with a canopy or tester over it. Such a bed was a wonderfully cozy place for two little girls to lie whispering and giggling in the dark before going to sleep at night. It was also a place they hated to climb out of when they had to get up to go to school at five o'clock in the morning. That was the hour school began in the warmer months.

Their school was a big, two-story building a short distance away on the corner of Second and Market Streets. It was called Dr. Ward's Academy and was attended by about a hundred and twenty boys and girls. Dr. John Ward was a minister, a learned, kindly gentleman, who believed, as many did at that time, that recitation should begin early in the morning.

This was fine in warm weather, for the soft Kentucky air was freshest around dawn and to walk along the streets in the new day was a delight. But it was another matter in winter, when the girls had to roll out from under their warm covers into an icy room, light a candle, and shiveringly dress by its feeble light. Sometimes they would have to walk those short blocks through sleet and snow.

One morning just before daybreak, as Mary was going to the school, she had an adventure. Elizabeth was not with her that morning and when Mary discovered a man was following her she was naturally frightened. She hurried her steps and so did the dark figure behind her. And oh, he had a club! Mary ran for her life.

She did not know the man was a night watchman named Flannigan who had just recently come to Lexington. When he spied a young girl going along the street at dawn carrying a bundle, he thought he had discovered an elopement. He could not allow that on his beat, so he zealously gave chase. Mary burst breathlessly into the schoolroom with Mr. Flannigan, club in hand, hot on her heels.

The school was struck dumb for a moment. Dr. Ward, his fine New England face stern with indignation, demanded an explanation. When watchman Flannigan said he thought Mary was a young lady running away from home to get married, the other children found it terribly funny and broke into a roar of laughter.

But Dr. Ward did not laugh. Mary had been badly frightened and she was one of his quickest and most responsive pupils. Elizabeth Humphreys, recalling later those evenings when she and Mary would bend their heads long and earnestly over their lessons, admitted that Mary always mastered hers first. Then she would take up her knitting needles, for, continued Elizabeth, "We were required to knit ten rounds of socks every evening."

Mrs. Todd was training the girls for marriage and the duties of a homemaker. Every housewife should knit socks. The opinion then was that domestic duties were all a girl needed to know. She would marry and raise a family, or, if she was so unlucky as to be an old maid, she would help her married sisters take care of their children. Only a "strong-minded" or "queer" female thought of anything so "unladylike" as a career of her own.

In spite of rules and restrictions and the lack of understanding between Mary and her stepmother, her days as a little girl had a happy pattern. To gather around a long breakfast table with a big family of children was in itself a lively way to begin a day. Especially when the children at that table were keen-witted, spunky, teasing young Todds.

There was Mary's oldest sister Elizabeth, a pretty girl whom they called Lizzie. The line of her life would in the future intertwine a great deal with Mary's. Then came her sister Frances, called Fanny, and her younger sister Ann. There were also her two brothers, Levi and George, an ever-increasing number of half sisters and half brothers, and, of course, Cousin Elizabeth Humphreys. Even though Mrs. Todd probably reminded them frequently that children should be seen and not heard, gaiety was irrepressible around that table while Old Nelson kept bringing in great platters of hot batter-cakes, waffles, corn muffins or spoon bread, and all the other bountiful dishes of an old-time Southern breakfast.

In the warm summer days the Todd children played endless games in the grassy yards of their father's and Grandmother Parker's homes. They explored a fascinating creek nearby where they waded and fished for minnows. This evidently resulted in some colds and sniffles, so that Mrs. Todd told them not to do it again. After that, when the children came in with their wet clothes betraying the fact they had been in the creek, they received a spanking. The Todd boys joked about it, saying that the little stream should not be called a "babbling" brook but a "blabbing" brook.

In the autumn they would go out to the woods to hunt nuts. They would shuffle along through the fallen leaves, making them rustle as much as possible. They would prick their fingers with chestnut burrs, or get them stained with the juice of walnut hulls, and at last, tired but triumphant, they would return home with loaded baskets.

Winter had its own special pattern. In the evenings the children sat before the big fireplace where hickory logs snapped and roared. There they cracked the nuts they had gathered the fall before, told stories, asked riddles, and played guessing games. The firelight was bright on their animated faces while their shadows danced on the floor behind them as the flames leaped up. The room would fill with the delicious smell of popping corn and apples roasting on the hearth.

All her life Elizabeth Humphreys loved to tell about those happy years she spent in the Todd home. She recalled how she and Mary shared certain incidents that were not important in themselves but were still like small bright highlights in her memory. There was the spring morning when they heard the peep of a baby turkey outside in the garden. No turkey was supposed to be in that garden and the girls rushed out to investigate. They must find that little fellow and feed and take care of him. They looked in the lilac hedge, the rose arbor, and the flower beds, but no feathered baby appeared.

"After hunting for some time," said Elizabeth, "we discovered the sound came from the honeysuckle vines which covered the latticed summer house at the end of the garden walk." Suddenly the little peeps had turned to the harsh notes of a jay bird. The two girls realized then that they had been fooled by a mockingbird. They caught the flash of the white feathers in his gray wings as he flew. Elizabeth added ruefully, " We had hunted half an hour for that turkey."

The grown-up Elizabeth also told about the excitement over the night-blooming cereus. This was a rare flower of the cactus family that had the peculiar habit of opening up at midnight. There was a saying that it bloomed only once in a hundred years. The Todds had a night-blooming cereus and there was great ado when it was found to have a bud.

Notes were taken to friends and neighbors inviting them to come to the opening. The girls were allowed to stay up until after twelve o'clock that night. Toward midnight hoop-skirted ladies and gentlemen in fancy shirts gathered around the plant, their expressions perhaps reflecting some of the wonder in the faces of the children. Mary and Elizabeth would not forget the breath-taking moments of that miracle by candlelight, when they saw the glistening white petals slowly unfold into the perfection of the large and fragrant blossom.

There was the bright June morning when the two

woke up with that special feeling you sometimes have that something nice is going to happen today. They were to take a journey; they were going to drive to Frankfort to visit Grandmother Humphreys for a whole week. They would wear their pretty frocks with the blue sashes, and their strapped slippers. Old Nelson in his blue coat with brass buttons would help them climb the three folding steps into the big Todd carriage and away they would go to the clopclop of the horses' hoofs down the turnpike or, as they called it, the pike.

Their hostess was Elizabeth's own grandmother and Mary's stepgrandmother. No matter how much Mary's opinions clashed with her stepmother's, she loved her bright-faced Grandmother Humphreys dearly.

It was fun to be with Grandmother Humphreys. She was not conventional and she did not believe a girl's interest should be limited to household duties. She was well educated, she knew French, and she delighted in reading all kinds of daring books. She thought slavery was wrong and she was going to free her slaves in her will. Moreover, she adored pretty clothes and she believed in having a good time. These were all views which Mary already shared or would grow to share. Mary said to Elizabeth, " If I can only be, when I am grown up, just like Grandmother Humphreys, I will be perfectly satisfied with myself."

The girls had many carriage journeys like this to visit their numerous kinsfolk. It was especially fun to go to a home in the country. But Mary did not have to go out of

Lexington to enjoy herself. When she walked along the quiet streets of that pleasant town, it held magic in her eyes. There were so many things dear to her because they were familiar: the church where she went to Sunday school, the fine homes set in deep lawns and flower gardens where lived people she knew and loved, the passing by of fine carriages with friends of her father leaning out to greet Mr. Todd's young daughter. Mary liked people and was interested in everything from bonnets to babies. She was by nature joyous with life.

One of her favorite people lived on Mill Street in a quaint, two-story brick building with an iron grill across the balcony on the upper story. This was Monsieur Giron, a short, stout little Frenchman who ran a famous confectionery shop. Elizabeth and Mary liked to stop in this shop on their way home from school, coming out richer with a spiced bun or hot ginger cake apiece. This made a good reason for visiting any shop, but in addition the girls saw such marvelous creations there.

In those days before telephones a bakery order was often given by a note. Elizabeth explained that she and Mary, when Mrs. Todd was planning one of her elaborate parties, always begged to take the written order to Monsieur Giron's so that "we might feast our eyes on the iced cakes decorated with garlands of pink sugar roses, or the bride's cakes with their fountains of clear, spun sugar, pyramiding in the center, veiling tiny fat cupids or little sugar brides."

Monsieur Giron, fastidiously dressed and with his

broad face beaming, would greet them in a courtly way that made them feel very important. He and Mary would have a lively exchange of conversation and she considered him one of her best friends.

But her supreme idol was Mr. Henry Clay, who lived out on the Richmond Pike on a big handsome estate called Ashland. There was glamor about Mr. Clay; he was a famous man over the nation. He had been a Senator and an important man in Washington. Mary was always thrilled when he came to her father's house as a guest. He was a striking figure, tall and slender, and a man with great charm. "Mr. Henry Clay," she once said, "is the handsomest man in town and has the best manners of anybody — except my father."

When Mary was about thirteen she paid Mr. Clay an unexpected call. It came about in this way. The week before an event had occurred which was very thrilling to her. A traveling show had come to town, a show that had a white pony who would do a little dance. The show ran out of money in Lexington and decided to sell the pony. Mary's father bought it.

Mary was excited beyond words when she was allowed to ride the pony. Perhaps she had to use a little sidesaddle; at least grown-up ladies then would never do anything so improper and shocking as to straddle a horse.

One day when Mary's stepmother was sick in bed and Mammy Sally was in charge, Mammy told Mary she could ride the pony up and down in front of the

Todd home for a little while. As Mary trotted up and down in the same spot, which was rather monotonous, it occurred to her what fun it would be to gallop down the Richmond Pike to Mr. Clay's house. She was always one to carry out an idea as soon as it occurred to her, so away she went. Arrived at Mr. Clay's home, she showed him the new pony and how the little fellow could dance. Mr. Clay smiled at the enthusiasm of Mr. Todd's pink-cheeked little girl and the pretty picture she made with the pony, then he filled her with rapture by inviting her to stay for dinner. He treated her with the same courtesy he would have shown a grown lady. That was a shining day for Mary, even if she did merit a scolding from Mammy.

The February after Mary's thirteenth birthday found the Todd home in a state of exciting preparations. Lizzie, her pretty older sister, was going to be married. Everyone was busy getting ready for guests, and Monsieur Giron's artistic hand was doubtless creating spun sugar fountains and fat cupids on his biggest wedding cake.

Mary loved parties and festivities of all kinds and took an eager interest in these activities. This was the first daughter's wedding in the family. It stirred Mary's quick emotions to see her sister, only several years older than herself, standing before the minister to take this tall, handsome young man for her husband. His name was Ninian Wirt Edwards and he came from way out West, from Illinois, where his father had been governor.

A wedding awakens long thoughts in a young girl. If

the time would come in the future when Mary would stand like this before a minister, what would he be like, the man at her side? She could not know that her sister's marriage was an essential link in the chain of her own destiny. At the very time this fine wedding was taking place in Kentucky, there was a tall young man living in a log-cabin village in Illinois called New Salem. He was poor, ill-dressed and uneducated, but he was struggling to learn and the pioneer people of New Salem had come to love him. His name was Abraham Lincoln.

Fate would contrive to bring this poor young man and the rich little girl together. There would be many turnings and twistings of events before the lines of their lives would cross, and many more strange happenings before those lines would join and run together. But in the marriage of Elizabeth Todd and Ninian Edwards, Fate had taken her first step toward this future. Now Fate would rest and wait until Mary had finished growing up.

· 3 ·

"Graces and Manners
of Young Ladies"

*A*FTER Elizabeth Todd's marriage, she went to Illinois to live and this left a vacancy in the household. But even so the home on Short Street was getting too crowded. Every year or so a new baby was arriving, another half brother or half sister for Mary, and it was plain to Mr. Todd that he would have to buy a bigger house.

The new home was a large and stately brick which stood on Main Street, its front-door steps coming down to the sidewalk itself. At the side was a beautiful garden with bright flowerbeds, rose arbor, and lilac hedge. A white gravel path ran through the clipped bluegrass ending at "the latticed summer house" which Elizabeth Humphreys mentioned in her story about the mockingbird. Mary, when she was grown and living far from Kentucky, would be homesick for this lovely spot. "I have been dreaming of our sweet old garden," she wrote. " I could still, in my mind's eye, see Elizabeth strolling with me on the garden walk."

Extensive grounds back of the new home contained a coachhouse for the big Todd carriage, a stable, and little cabins for Mammy Sally, Old Nelson, and the other slaves. And to the joy of the Todd boys, the "blabbing brook" ran right through the rear of the lot.

In addition to needing a roomier house, there may have been another reason why Mr. and Mrs. Todd were glad to move their family from the house on Short Street. Directly across from it was a place where slaves were kept while waiting to be sold, and this created scenes not pleasant to look upon. But cruel signs of slavery were on all sides in Lexington. There were the auction block and whipping post on the public square in the center of town. In the new home on Main Street, Mary often saw long lines of dejected slaves, chained together, passing by on their way to the slave markets of the deep South.

One day she and Cousin Elizabeth heard a terrible story. Some cruel people in New Orleans had chained their slaves in the attic and then set the house afire. The slaves were rescued in time but the hideous intent of the owners was evident. "We were horrified," said Elizabeth, "and talked of nothing else for days." The two girls finally decided that if such cruelties were possible, slavery must be a monstrous wrong. They knew the Todd slaves were treated kindly and as for selling them, "I love them all!" cried Mary passionately. "I would feel as if I were selling a member of my own family." Influenced no doubt by the fact that Grandmother

Humphreys and Mr. Henry Clay both believed that arrangements should be made to set all slaves free, Mary herself grew into this belief.

Mammy Sally one night told her and Elizabeth a deep secret, one they must never mention to anyone. A special mark, said Mammy, was on the fence in the alley at the rear of the Todd home. Sometimes a runaway slave, trying to get to the Ohio River and cross it to a free state, would slip through the alley. That mark told the hungry, hunted creature that the slaves at that house would give him food. He would then creep to the little cabins at the back of the lot and knock at a door, where he would be taken in, fed, and comforted.

Once Mary and Elizabeth overheard a knocking and Mammy told them it was a runaway slave. The two warmhearted little girls were on fire with sympathy. With her usual impulsiveness Mary wanted to take the food out herself. But Mammy restrained her, saying, "No, honey," and reminded her that a white person would frighten the poor fugitive. Only a black hand could reach out to give him the bacon and cornbread. "We kept Mammy's secret," said Elizabeth, who told the story later, "and though we often listened, did not again hear the knocking; but from that time our ears were keyed for any tales of oppression."

So slavery became a distressing puzzle to Mary, as it was to a great many people throughout the nation at that time. What would the young girl have felt if she could have known that the man who would one day stand with her before a minister to be married would also be the man who would set all these slaves free!

Though Mary loved Mammy Sally and the others so dearly, she and the rest of the Todd children liked to play little pranks on them. Mammy had her own resourceful way of discouraging such behavior. She impressed upon her "chil'en" that jay birds went to hell every Friday night and told the devil all the naughty things they had done in the past week.

Mammy's rich imagination painted a vivid picture of the jay bird's reporting at the "bad place." She described the big and awful devil standing there with horns on his head and a long pea-green tail. Nearby at a table which held a big book was a little devil sitting on a stool so high that his tail did not even "tech the flo'." Mr. Jay Bird twittered in Mr. Devil's ear that Mary hid Mammy's slippers when she took them off in the garden to rest her feet. "Old Man Satan" bellowed to the small devil, "Write that down in yo' big book, little son." Mr. Jay disclosed that Elizabeth helped Mary in all her "mis*chee*vous doin's." "Old Man Satan" yelled to write that down "keerful." It was revealed and recorded that little Ann Todd "hollered when Mammy curled her hair." The fact that Mary put salt instead of sugar in Mammy's coffee was doubtless written down in capital letters.

Mary liked to tease Mammy by arguing that the devil's tail could not have been pea-green. It surely was a black tail. But Mammy stood her ground firmly on that and all the other particulars. Even though the children quickly grew big enough to know it was all make-believe, it is a safe guess that jay birds were not exactly popular around the Todd yard and garden. The flicker of brilliant blue wings from tree to shrub or the harsh call of "Jay! Jay!" may have stopped more than one small iniquity! It was just as well not to take any chances!

The little Todds were a bit cautious about playing tricks on Chaney, or, as they called her, "Aunt Chaney," the cook. The children followed the gentle Southern custom of calling older Negro servants "aunt" and "uncle." Aunt Chaney was a marvelous cook but was quick-tempered and cross. Any suggestion of teasing her was likely to be followed by the banging of pans and kettles and orders to get out of the kitchen. Mary had learned, however, that a tactful gift such as a red and yellow bandanna handkerchief to tie around her head had a wonderfully soothing effect on Aunt Chaney's crossness.

After Mary finished the preparatory course at Dr. Ward's Academy, she was sent to a select boarding school conducted by a cultured Frenchwoman, Madame Victorie Mentelle. She lived there five days out of the week. Madame Mentelle's school was a rambling, ivy-covered house out on the Richmond Pike just across from Ashland, the home of Mr. Henry Clay. Every

Monday morning Old Nelson would help Mary into the Todd carriage and drive her out to the school and on Friday afternoons he would call for her again.

Madame Mentelle's was what has been called a "finishing school," a school to prepare young girls for entering society. Mary was now about fourteen and ready for this training. It was said that Madame Mentelle "spared no pains with the graces and manners of young Ladies submitted to her care." These young girls would soon be attending stately balls. Madame therefore instructed them "in the latest and most fashionable Cotillions, Round & Hop Waltzes" and many other dances, including one with the intriguing title of "Beautiful Circassian Circle."

In the candlelit winter evenings Monsieur Mentelle would play the violin while the teen-age girls went through the figures of these dances under Madame's supervision. Mary loved dancing and was good at it and those were joyous evenings for her. She fitted happily into the school routine and soon found warm, affectionate companionships with the other girls. She probably already knew them as the daughters of her father's friends. When Madame sent her little flock to bed at night, there were doubtless whispered confidences, a bit of mischief-plotting, and girlish giggles. Looking back later, Mary said that Madame Mentelle's was a real home to her, a happy home.

French was considered a valuable social accomplishment at the time and of course Madame Mentelle was beautifully qualified to teach it. The girls were required to speak French at the school. The day came when Mary, home for the weekend, dropped in at the confectionery on Mill Street and began to talk to her good friend Monsieur Giron in his own language. What fun that was! You can imagine how the eyes of the little Frenchman sparkled and what a voluble, rapturous reply he made.

Soon they were able to hold long conversations in French, for there was nothing superficial in Mary's knowledge of the language. She became at home in it and would find it useful when one day she would live for a while in France.

Mary had been at Madame Mentelle's for two years when the schoolmistress decided that the girls should put on a French play which they had been studying. Mary was thrilled when the leading role was given to her. She delighted in dramatics and had an instinct for acting, a gift that was evident when she told a story. She made the story come alive with her changing expressions and gestures and she could mimic other people to perfection.

The play was to be given on a Friday afternoon and Mary invited Elizabeth Humphreys to come out to the school for the event. Evidently Cousin Elizabeth did not attend Madame Mentelle's. She was not the daughter of the prominent Mr. Todd but only his wife's niece, who was making her home with them. Elizabeth was missing the warm, exciting companionship with Mary and looked forward eagerly to the weekends, when she would be home. "How I hated to see her go back to school on Monday morning," said Elizabeth.

The play was quite an occasion. Each pupil was allowed to invite a guest and there was to be a party after the play. Early that afternoon Old Nelson brought the carriage around and Cousin Elizabeth, accompanied by Mary Jane, a young slave girl, climbed in. Mary Jane carried a huge box which contained a cake made by Aunt Chaney, a contribution to the party refreshments.

"Mary was waiting impatiently at the door as we drove up," said Elizabeth, "and flew at me like a whirlwind. I had not seen her for a week and I thought she had grown prettier during that time, she looked so dainty in her fresh white muslin frock and silk sash!" Her cheeks were pink, her blue eyes "were sparkling with excitement, her pretty chestnut curls were bright and glossy," and she was chattering away in French. The little slave girl, hearing "Miss Mary" getting off such outlandish talk, shied "like a skittish colt" and was in danger of dropping the cakebox!

Elizabeth had seen her cousin take a small part in a play before and had sat trembling for fear she would forget her lines. But this time, watching Mary sweeping across the stage and throwing herself into her role, the loyal Elizabeth said she "was thrilled with her talent" and thought she "was the star actress of the school." The play was a great success and it is safe to assume that Aunt Chaney's cake, which was served afterwards, was a success too.

Four years at Madame Mentelle's, happy years punctuated with small triumphs like this, went by. Mary finished at the "finishing school." She was now an attractive young woman of eighteen. She had developed a petite but prettily rounded figure and had come into the glory of wearing the hoop skirts she had so longed for at ten.

The year of her eighteenth birthday she became the eldest daughter at home, for her sister Fanny went out to Springfield, Illinois, to live with their sister Elizabeth, Mrs. Ninian Edwards. The number of Todd daughters at Lexington did not diminish, however; it was in that same year that Mary's little half sister Emilie, whom she was to love so dearly, was born.

Letters came from the two sisters in Illinois, the quaint letters of that day which had no stamps or envelopes but were closely written pages folded and fastened with a seal. The receiver paid the postage, which for a long distance could be as much as twenty-five cents a single sheet. Mr. Todd gladly paid for word from his older daughters, and learned that they wanted Mary to come out to visit them.

Mary did go to see her sisters in Illinois in the summer of 1837, but there is no record of the details of that visit. Fate could have contrived then to have her meet a tall young lawyer who had moved to the town in April of that year, but Fate was apparently in no hurry. Mary probably heard the name of this young man, Abraham Lincoln, as he had become the junior law partner of her cousin, John Todd Stuart, in Springfield. But she did not meet him then.

She returned to Lexington, where she was now "in society." Society in Lexington was very active, with sumptuous dinners, receptions, and entertainments of all kinds. Mary had beaux who escorted her to elaborate dances held in the big ballroom over Monsieur Giron's confectionery. No hint of romance developed, however. This girl was destined to give her heart to one man only and to love him with a great, single devotion all the rest of her life.

Mary took, as always, a delighted interest in parties and people, but much as she enjoyed them, they were not quite enough to fill her days. She went back to her dear Dr. Ward for guidance in further study. She loved literature, especially poetry, and Dr. Ward took her far into the kingdom of books. With an excellent memory, she had already learned enough poetry to recite it by the hour, if need be. Her letters were sprinkled with quotations from Shakespeare and other poets.

Her stepmother probably had little sympathy with Mary's literary explorations. Conventional people then called a girl a "bluestocking" if she ventured to have intellectual interests outside of "woman's sphere." Such interests, in their opinion, bordered on the "unladylike."

Now that she was grown, Mary's relationship with her stepmother disturbed her more than ever. The girl suffered because it seemed clear to her she was not wanted in the home of her own father, whom she loved.

It made her feel, to use her own word, "desolate." The ailing, overburdened Mrs. Todd was evidently anxious to get the stepchildren off her hands.

They were leaving as soon as they could. Mary's brother George said later that Mr. Todd, who was a kind father, was distressed that the stepmother's attitude was driving away from home his children by his first marriage.

Out in Illinois Fanny had married a doctor of Springfield, Dr. William Wallace. Now Mary's sister Elizabeth had room for her to come. She wrote inviting Mary to come live with her. It seemed best to go.

It was hard for Mary to leave Lexington, which held so many people she loved — her father, her sister Ann, her two brothers and the whole stairsteps of half brothers and half sisters. How could she part from little Emilie, now a beautiful little girl going on three? She made the rounds saying good-by to all her friends, who suddenly seemed more dear. How could she do without Monsieur Giron, Mr. Henry Clay, and all the others when she moved to Illinois?

The packing and preparations were completed. One October morning in 1839, after a tearful farewell to Mammy Sally and Aunt Chaney and hugs and kisses to all the family, Mary climbed into the Todd carriage and Old Nelson drove her to the little depot at Mill and Water Streets. Railroads were very few and primitive then, but Lexington was proud to have a little train it called "the Nottaway." It stood now on the narrow

Picture above by courtesy of William H. Townsend; picture below by courtesy of the Illinois State Historical Library

Two Houses Important to Mary

Above is Dr. Ward's Academy in Lexington, Kentucky, where Mary went to school. Below is the Edwards home in Springfield, Illinois, where Mr. Lincoln courted Mary and where they were married.

track, a tiny engine with one coach for passengers. Old Nelson helped the engineer load on "Miss Mary's" baggage and the girl entered the single car.

The train started with a jolt and was soon rattling down Water Street and out into the Kentucky countryside. The first stage of the long journey had begun. Mary would not make her home again under her father's roof. She was on her way to meet her destiny in Illinois.

· 4 ·

Enter Mr. Lincoln

*M*ARY would be traveling at least a week before she reached Springfield. The little train would carry her only the twenty-odd miles to Frankfort and that would be the end of trains on the trip. Rivers were the great highways of travel in those days and at Frankfort it would be possible to board a steamboat on the Kentucky River.

Mary always loved a journey and going places on a river boat had interests all its own. These big boats were like bright-colored floating palaces, with white railings around the several decks, one above the other, and the decorated, gilded little pilothouse perched like a jewel box on top. There was endless fascination in watching the giant paddle wheel, which filled the air with shining drops of water as it turned and left a long white trail of foam behind the boat.

The friendly girl could stand at the rail chatting with the other passengers who had gathered there to watch the boatmen tie up at each little river town. The people of the town always came down to welcome the boat, and there would be loading and unloading and exchange of news. As the steamboat moved slowly along she could see new countrysides and different people on the banks. Strange, picturesque river craft were constantly passing by. The drama of river life was ever changing.

At night lying in her bunk she would be lulled to sleep by the vibration of the engine, which was on the lowest deck.

Springfield, Illinois, was northwest of Lexington, Kentucky, but Mary traveled a long way south on the wide Ohio River. The boat must go down the Ohio to the point at Cairo, Illinois, where it flowed into the mighty Mississippi. If the girl looked down from the deck at the right moment, she could see the line where the two rivers joined and the great swirls of the muddy Mississippi made a vast pattern of tawny plumes in the clear water of the Ohio. There the boat changed its course to the northwest. Now its decks trembled more than ever with the throb of the engine as it labored to push the boat up the Mississippi against the powerful current. This was much harder than coming down-stream on the Ohio.

About a week had passed since she left Lexington when Mary arrived at St. Louis. She was still two days' journey by stagecoach from Springfield, two days of jolting along unbelievably rough roads by day and spending the night at some primitive tavern. She was now in Illinois, where the prairie land was flat and the soil was rich and black.

The journey was near its end. The girl, seeing landmarks which she remembered from her visit of two years before, doubtless knew when to watch for the church spires of Springfield. The stagecoach driver probably whipped up his horses for an impressive entrance into the little town and drew the reins with a flourish in front of a two-story wooden building called the Globe Tavern. A large bell on its roof began to ring as the coach halted; it was a signal for the stablemen to come running from the rear of the inn to take care of the horses. Mary, gazing at this unprepossessing tavern, could not dream it would be the birthplace of her first baby.

Perhaps Elizabeth and Ninian Edwards met her at this tavern. At all events, Mary was soon at their home and was being warmly welcomed into the family group. There were embracings and kisses between the sisters and everyone doubtless talked at once wanting to know the news from the old home in Kentucky. One thing Mary must have missed, however, in that arrival. There were no comforting Negro house servants in the background beaming their welcome. Illinois did not have slaves. Servants of any kind were hard to get and housekeeping was much more difficult than in Kentucky.

In addition to her two married sisters, Elizabeth Edwards and Frances Wallace, Mary had a number of kinsfolk in Springfield. Her father's brother, Dr. John Todd, was a physician with a fine home and family. A leading lawyer of the town, John Todd Stuart, was her first cousin. "Cousin John" had taken a junior law partner in his office two years before, a young man named Lincoln.

Mary settled into her new home with her usual lively interest. There were many things that contrasted with the life she had left behind. The Edwards house was on a hill somewhat out from the more built-up center of town, and while one family, the Leverings, lived near them, there was not so much passing by as on Main Street in Lexington. Still, sister Elizabeth had married into the top social circle and she entertained a great deal, so that many people climbed that hill to the Edwards home. It was a fine home, richly furnished, but such homes were very few in Springfield. It was almost a frontier town and seemed raw and new after the beautiful scenes and homesteads of an older place like Lexington.

Never, however, was a little town more alive than Springfield. A wonderful thing had happened to it not long before. It had become the state capital of Illinois. When the news first came, its citizens, in joyous celebration, had danced around a huge bonfire on the public square which was the center of town. Springfield was a young town in a young part of the country and it was filled with young people.

The men so far outnumbered the women that at dances there were never half enough girls to go around.

The arrival of an attractive girl like Mary was news that spread rapidly. It at once increased the number of young men who climbed the hill to sit in the Edwards parlor. Soon the Edwards home became the center of a lively, well-read, poetry-quoting group of young people who called themselves "The Coterie." They were intensely interested in matters like picnics, parties, balls, sleigh rides, romance, and weddings and they had a wonderful time together. Mary entered joyfully into all activities and soon the members of the Coterie were calling her by the nickname "Molly."

Warm friendships were essential to this girl. She especially felt the need of a close, loved companion. Elizabeth Humphreys had been her little-girl running mate but now Elizabeth was far away. It therefore seemed providential when a lovely girl came from the East that same fall to spend the winter at the Levering home next door. The girl was Mr. Levering's sister, Mercy Levering.

Mary and Mercy were soon congenial and devoted friends. Mercy was a gentle girl who always remembered the rules of propriety and never took any chances that she might be called "unladylike." She was an excellent companion for Mary, who was a bit too excitable and impulsive for her own good. Mercy even had the puritanical feeling that enjoying oneself too much was "frivolous." To be accused of "frivolity" in those days was just too bad. Mercy would scold Mary for her innocent pleasure in clothes and parties and urge her to turn her thoughts "from earthly vanities." Mary replied she wished she could, she knew such pleasures were not the most important things but it was her nature to be cheerful. "My feelings & hopes," she said, "are all so sanguine."

In coming to Springfield, Mary had not escaped from hampering opinions. Her sister Elizabeth thought also that she was inclined to be too frivolous. As the oldest sister she had Mary's welfare at heart according to her own ideas, but they were strict and conventional ideas very much like those of their stepmother.

Mary ran up against these opinions in an adventure which she and Mercy shared not long after they became such good friends. Springfield had almost nothing in the way of pavement and after a hard or prolonged rain the walks and roadways were a sea of mud. Even buggies sometimes mired down in the crossings around the public square. Men managed to get around in high boots but girls in hoop skirts that touched the floor were forced to stay at home. If they lifted those skirts and showed their ankles they would be called unladylike in those strait-laced days.

A continued rain had kept Mary housebound for days. She very much disliked being shut in, especially when she wanted to go to town. Possibly she had some shopping to do, some ribbon or yard goods to buy for her sewing. Shopping would always be a favorite occupation of hers.

How could she manage it? She had a sudden idea. Just

as once she had thought of using willow switches for hoops, now she planned to make shingles a substitute for a sidewalk. She would take a bundle of shingles and drop them one at a time in front of her and step from shingle to shingle to keep out of the mud. She would ask Mercy Levering to go with her.

The two girls, "both elegantly attired," started out. They made their way shinglewise down the hill and crossed the bridge over a little stream. It was about six blocks from their doors to the business section around "the square," as they called it. Soon, however, it was clear the plan was not going to work very well. Springfield's sticky black mud could swallow much larger and stouter objects than a few thin little pieces of wood; the shingles simply did not keep them out of the mud.

But now they were some blocks from home, tired and bedraggled. How were they going to get back? Just as they were discussing this question, there came along the roadway a horse-drawn two-wheeled cart called a dray. Its driver, a little man named Ellis Hart, did hauling for many people in the town and evidently Mary knew him. She had another bright idea — she would get Ellis Hart to drive them home in his dray.

Mercy was shocked. Ladies should never make themselves conspicuous in public and anything more conspicuous than two "elegantly attired" young ladies being hauled through the streets of Springfield in a two-wheeled cart would be hard to imagine. It would create a sensation. Mercy felt sure her brother, at whose home

Attire for a Dray Ride

This is what the "elegantly attired" lady was wearing when
Mary took her dray ride. No wonder that

> *Up flew windows, out popped heads,*
> *To see this Lady gay*
> *In silken cloak and feathers white*
> *A riding on a dray.*

she was visiting, would be very much upset if she did such a thing. She declined to get into the dray.

Mary was probably none too patient with these delicate, ladylike scruples in a matter that seemed to her to call for good common sense. There was no harm in riding with the little drayman and she wanted to go home without getting any more mud on her skirts. She climbed into the dray and was driven off. The account does not state how Mercy got back to the hill — it leaves her stuck in the mud or possibly wading home through it.

Perhaps Mary hoped she would not meet anyone she knew on the way but she did. Worse still, it was a member of the Coterie, a pleasant gentleman named Dr. E. H. Merryman. He stared in astonishment and then called out to ask what she was doing there. She made a spirited and cheerful reply. Much amused at her independence and given to verse-making, as many in the Coterie were, he wrote a jingle about it which was passed around and laughed over in the group.

> *As I walked out on Monday last*
> *A wet and muddy day*
> *'Twas there I saw a pretty lass*
>   *A riding on a dray . . .*
> *Quoth I, sweet lass, what do you there*
> *Said she good lack a day*
> *I had no coach to take me home*
>   *So I'm riding on a dray.*

Enter Mr. Lincoln

As Mercy had foreseen, people were shocked.

> *Up flew windows, out popped heads,*
> *To see this Lady gay*
> *In silken cloak and feathers white*
> *A riding on a dray.*

Dr. Merryman, like most members of the Coterie, enjoyed teasing. Mary was inclined to be plump and her friends delighted in poking fun at her about it. Having in mind the way in which the little drayman unloaded his cart by opening it at the back and rolling off the casks and barrels, Dr. Merryman with a twinkle continued his poem:

> *At length arrived at Edwards' gate*
> *Hart backed the usual way*
> *And taking out the iron pin*
> *He rolled her off the dray.*

When Mary entered the house it is safe to assume that her sister Elizabeth gave her a good scolding. How could she make such a spectacle of herself? The whole town would be talking about it. Had she forgotten she was a Todd and the sister-in-law of Ninian Edwards?

It was an age of snobbish class distinctions and the Todds and Edwardses belonged to the "upper class" which felt very superior to the "lower classes." This aristocratic attitude was to prove a very serious "hampering opinion" in romantic events that were soon to follow.

I Mary

One evening Mary dressed herself with the delightful feeling of anticipation which a girl has when she is going to a dance. It was a cotillion and very probably the one known to have taken place at Springfield's most pretentious hotel, the American House, in December. As she carefully arranged her hair and put on her most festive dress Mary had no inkling, as no girl ever has, that Fate had decided the time had come for her to meet her future husband.

Soon she entered the big candlelit ballroom, where other members of the Coterie were assembling, dressed in their party best. There were new faces, as the meeting of the state legislature in December brought many gentlemen back to town. Stately introductions were being made. Suddenly Mary was aware that a tall, lean gentleman was being presented to her, a Mr. Lincoln. The unusual length of his legs was emphasized by the slim trousers then in style. With these narrow trousers went a long-tailed coat, a satin vest cut low to display a great deal of fine shirt, and a muffler-like tie called a stock made into a small bow in front.

Mary, lifting her eyes to this gentleman's face, may have thought at first that it was rather homely. She saw dark, unruly hair, strong, rugged features and a pair of deep-set gray eyes gazing back at her with great interest. This must be Cousin John's law partner of whom she had heard.

Years afterwards Mary delighted to tell what happened at the dance after they met. Mr. Lincoln, a bit shy and ill at ease, "at last came awkwardly forward and said: 'Miss Todd, I want to dance with you in the worst way.'" At this point in the story she would add with a little chuckle, "And he surely did."

In that first dance together both of them made some discoveries. Mary undoubtedly met his shyness with her usual friendly talkativeness and found out when that "homely" countenance lit up with response and feeling it was one of the most interesting faces she had seen. He was big and yet so gentle. There was something about him that drew her to him.

Mr. Lincoln was making his discoveries also. He was more than a foot taller than this dainty girl, so that he could look down on her bright chestnut hair and see the sweep of long lashes against the pink curve of her cheek. He had a way of saying droll things with a twinkle and when Mary laughed he found out she had dimples. Her hand when it touched his in the dance seemed very small and white against his great brown fist.

He was well acquainted with her brother-in-law, Ninian Edwards, as they were in the state legislature together. So it came about that soon Mr. Lincoln was frequently seen sitting on the slippery horsehair chairs or sofa in the Edwards parlor. If this meant that he was getting especially interested in Miss Mary Todd, he was destined to have rivals. Other gentlemen of the Coterie were getting into the habit of sitting in those chairs too.

· 5 ·

"Bargains" and "Beaux"

*O*NE of Mary's beaux was a gentleman named Stephen A. Douglas. His name, like that of Abraham Lincoln, was destined to be written into history. Mr. Douglas had a massive head, strong face, vibrant voice, and a personality suggestive of great force. Because this impressive head and body were set on short legs he was nicknamed the "Little Giant."

He was a keen and gifted young man and Mary always liked "brainy" people. Besides, the two had a good time when they were together. Once when he found her making a wreath of flowers (she loved to place flowers in her hair), she dared him to wear it on his head as they walked down the street. Mr. Douglas was not easily abashed. He put the wreath on that powerful head of his — where it looked very ridiculous — and away they went laughing gaily.

As Mary's first winter in Illinois passed the milestone of New Year's Day and turned into the spring of 1840, a third gentleman was thinking a good deal about little Miss Todd. His name was Edwin B. Webb. He was a lawyer of some prominence, eighteen years older than Mary, and a widower with two little children. He may have noticed the girl's expression when she cuddled a baby in her arms or entered delightedly into a game with older youngsters. It was clear to anyone that she loved children dearly. Mr. Webb was to become more and more convinced that year that this attractive young woman would make him a fine second wife. Romantic complications were increasing for Mary.

By summer she had discovered much more about Mr. Lincoln. They saw each other at the various parties of the Coterie and when he called at the Edwards home. She soon found out that he, like Mr. Douglas, had a keen, thoughtful mind, but there was a great difference between them. Mr. Lincoln sometimes pronounced his words as people do in the backwoods; he might, for example, say "cheer" when he meant "chair." But he read a great deal and loved books just as she did. Perhaps he came to tell her by and by how, when he was growing up on a pioneer's farm in the wilderness with less than a year of going to school in all, he had hungered for books. There were so few books within his reach that once later he had walked miles to borrow a grammar because he wanted so much to educate himself.

He had been born in a log cabin and lived in log cabins until he had come to Springfield. In the bright, self-assured Coterie he was sometimes smiled at because of his countrified speech and ways. He felt this and his face would be wistful because he wanted so much to feel that he belonged in the group. He had had no chance before to learn the ways of society and he was too poor to get the finest clothes.

Mary herself probably smiled at his awkwardness at first. But as she learned more about him she became very sympathetic. They found many topics on which they were congenial. They could not only talk about literary matters together and quote favorite verses to each other; Mr. Lincoln, who was tremendously interested in public affairs, would talk about politics with her.

This was wonderful! Mary had a natural taste for the workings of politics but here again she was up against a hampering opinion. The prevailing masculine belief at that time was that girls should stay strictly in the "woman's sphere" of domestic duties. They should not bother their weak little female minds with weighty subjects like politics but leave such things to intelligent creatures like men! Mary was taking a keen interest in the presidential election which was coming up that fall, but she felt it was necessary to apologize for that interest.

Mr. Lincoln did not think it was unfeminine for a girl to talk about politics or literature. He liked it. Perhaps one reason Mary was drawn to him was that he was not always trying, with an air of disapproval, to shoo her back into woman's sphere.

They could not have discussed political matters very long without mentioning the statesman Henry Clay.

"Bargains" and "Beaux"

What a thrill it must have been to Mary when she discovered that Mr. Lincoln's political idol was her own beloved Mr. Clay. She always spoke rapidly but her words must have tumbled over themselves as she told Mr. Lincoln what a friend of hers Mr. Clay was. She could describe his tall, slender figure and deep-set gray eyes, which, if she came to think of it, were not unlike Mr. Lincoln's own.

The young lawyer was delighted to hear Mary talk on any subject. Mrs. Edwards described what she saw as she glanced into the parlor when he came calling: Mr. Lincoln sitting there "charmed" and "fascinated" with "Mary's wit" and "culture." He would listen and "gaze on her as if drawn by some superior power, irresistibly so." It is a very good description of a man falling in love.

This is the way matters stood that summer when Mary left Springfield to make a visit to the family of her uncle, Judge David Todd, in Columbia, Missouri. Uncle David had a daughter Ann about Mary's age and the two girls were soon going to dances and taking excursions and having a grand time. Then something unexpected happened. Who should turn up in town but Mr. Lincoln of Illinois! It seems that he had some matter of business that had brought him out to Missouri! He stayed over Sunday, saw much of Mary, and attended church with her and her uncle's family.

A young man does not usually go to so much trouble to see a girl unless he is courting her in earnest. By the time he left Columbia, Mary had some serious thinking to do.

On this visit she wrote Mercy Levering a letter which has been preserved. It is a wonderful thing to read this letter written more than century ago. The years between vanish and you can listen directly to Mary as she tells what she was thinking on that July day long past.

It is a long, affectionate letter to her "Dearest Merce," a letter filled for the most part with lively chatter about the fun she and Cousin Ann are having. But she strikes a different note when she says she has something to tell Merce which will surprise her. It is about certain letters she has received since leaving Springfield and "I *must confess* they were entirely *unlooked for*. This is *between ourselves*, my dearest, but of this more anon." Had these unexpected letters been from Mr. Lincoln, saying he was coming to Missouri? Mary evidently has something confidential she is aching to tell her friend but she hesitates to write it. "How much I wish you were near," she goes on, "ever have I found yours a congenial heart."

It is clear that something has turned Mary's thoughts to what lies ahead for her. She makes hinting remarks all around the subject, using, as people did in that day, an excess of commas. "Every day I am convinced this is a stranger world we live in, the *past* as the future is to me a mystery." She says that ". . . mine I fancy is to be a quiet lot, and happy indeed will I be, if it is, only cast near those, I *so dearly love*." If she were to marry a poor man like Mr. Lincoln most people would predict that hers was destined to be a very quiet lot. The second part of her statement contained a fundamental truth about Mary: love would always be the thing she put first. It was what mattered most of all to her.

Mary tells her friend she has acquired still another beau since coming to Missouri. He is "an agreeable lawyer & grandson of *Patrick Henry — what an honor!*" He wants Mary to marry him and stay in Columbia. "Uncle and others think, he surpasses his *noble ancestor* in *talents*, yet Merce I love him not, & my hand will never be given, where my heart is not." This gentleman was rather odd and in telling of this Mary added, "My beaux have *always* been *hard bargains* at any rate." The girl could have foreseen that if she decided to marry Mr. Lincoln, her aristocratic sister Elizabeth would consider that a very "hard bargain" for a Todd.

With her various beaux thus occupying her mind, Mary came back from Missouri to Springfield. Mercy Levering was still away and she missed her dreadfully. She wanted someone to talk with confidentially. Her sisters Elizabeth and Frances would never do — they were cold and critical about Mr. Lincoln. As the fall social activities began he and Mr. Webb both were frequently to be seen calling in the Edwards parlor.

A member of the Coterie wrote Mercy in October that Miss Todd did not seem "as merry and joyous as usual." Then, in the middle of December, Mary herself wrote a long letter to "my ever dear Merce," a letter which has many hints that she was in a disturbed frame of mind. The reason is not hard to guess; any girl is troubled who finds herself caring deeply for a man of whom her family does not approve. For by December, Mr. Lincoln's homely face was becoming the dearest face in the world to Mary, the face which mattered most.

Mary's letter, of course, gave all the latest news in full detail. She told Mercy that a friend of theirs was to be married soon. "I am pleased she is about perpetrating the *crime* of *matrimony*," she added, "I think she will be much happier." Why should Mary speak of marriage as a "crime"? Had her sister Elizabeth been remarking it would be a crime if she married a man of such humble origin as Mr. Lincoln?

Mary's letter showed plainly she was pondering the subject of marriage. Two friends of hers and Mercy's had recently become brides. One of them "appears to be enjoying all the sweets of married life," she wrote, but the other one seemed much more sober since her wedding. Mary asked the question, "Why is it that married folks always become so serious?"

There was another sign that she was worrying. She said she was losing weight but added quickly that she still had "quite a sufficiency."

She spoke freely to Mercy about Mr. Webb's wooing, saying that he "dances attendance very frequently." But she said nothing about Mr. Lincoln's courting of her, perhaps because she was self-conscious about that mat-

ter. She mentioned casually that he, like some other gentlemen in the Coterie, had some new clothes and that
he was to be one of a party of eight or nine of her friends
with whom she was planning a two-day jaunt to Jack-
sonville "next week." Mr. Webb was going too. She
added, "We are watching the clouds most anxiously
trusting it may snow, so we may have a sleigh ride. —
Will it not be pleasant?"

Just what happened on that jaunt can only be guessed.
Perhaps, away from Mrs. Edwards's disapproving eyes,
Mr. Lincoln had a chance to come to an understanding
with Mary. Where it happened and what the two said
to each other on that occasion is not known. But it is
known definitely that Mary did not let Mr. Lincoln's
limited means, backwoods upbringing, or her sister's disapproval stand between her and the man she loved. By
the end of December, Mary Todd and Abraham Lincoln
had confessed their love to each other, had become engaged, and had begun to make their plans to be married.

· 6 ·

"The Course of True Love Never Did Run Smooth"

*T*o a girl with Mary's quickly soaring spirit the engagement undoubtedly brought a great lift of happiness. She and Mr. Lincoln loved each other! She did not call him "Abe" or "Abraham." According to the formal custom of the time he was always "Mr. Lincoln" to her.

It may have been especially sweet to her to know she had become necessary to his happiness. She had grown up feeling she was not wanted by her stepmother. In Springfield her sister Elizabeth had a critical attitude toward her lighthearted and democratic ways. But this gentle, magnetic man loved her for herself, just as she was, and she gave him her whole affectionate heart in return.

What had happened must have been equally strange and wonderful to him. He was a homeless man in Springfield and had known little except hardship and loneliness up to the time he came there. He considered that he was, to use his own words, "a poor nobody then," although he was struggling hard to make something of himself. It meant everything to him that this girl, at whom he had been gazing in spellbound fashion on his calls, not only gave him her devotion but also believed confidently in his talents and his future.

There is a saying that "The course of true love never did run smooth." It was to prove so with Mary and Abraham.

Complications appeared right away. Elizabeth Edwards made it increasingly evident that she was very much opposed to their marriage. She felt that Mary, if she married Mr. Lincoln, would be marrying "beneath her." The opposition of the Edwardses carried weight because Mary, living at their house, was in a sense under their care and control. Mr. Edwards considered that he was her guardian. Fathers and guardians had heavy-handed rights in regard to a girl's marriage then.

As soon as Mary and Mr. Lincoln began to talk over their plans, his limited means stuck out like a sore thumb. He could not give her a home at first; they would have to live at a boardinghouse. He was not only poor — he was in debt.

Abraham Lincoln had a very tender conscience. He had said several years before this, "I want in all cases to do right, and most particularly so, in all cases with women." Would it be right to ask this girl to face hardships she knew nothing about? She had always lived in well-to-do homes, had pretty clothes, and was used to handsome entertaining. She was more than nine years younger than he was and impulsive; was he taking advantage of her inexperience? He would be so happy married to her provided she was happy too. But if her bright, joyous spirit became dimmed by his poverty, he would be utterly miserable. He wrestled with this problem without finding the answer.

It was apparently about this time that an incident happened which hurt him deeply and greatly increased his doubts. As Mary's niece told the story, Mr. Lincoln had a date to take Mary to a dance. Getting deeply absorbed in thought, he forgot about the passing of time and did not remember his appointment until after the hour.

Meanwhile the girl, when he did not come, went on to the party without him. She was humiliated and angry that he had forgotten her. When he came to himself and realized he was late he hurried after her, first to the Edwards home and then to the party itself. As he entered the door he saw her dancing with her beau Mr. Douglas. She had seen him enter but pretended she had not. Instead, for Mr. Lincoln's benefit, she put on an elaborate show of flirting with Mr. Douglas, looking at him doubtless with flattering eyes as if she thought he was the most wonderful man she knew. (Mr. Douglas probably wondered what had brought him into such sudden favor!) Deeply hurt and jealous, Mr. Lincoln left the hall without speaking to her.

He was already terribly sensitive about having so little to offer Mary. Now he felt worse than ever. Perhaps she did not really love him after all, perhaps it would make her happier to marry Mr. Douglas or Mr. Webb, who were better established than he was and could give her more. Maybe Mr. and Mrs. Edwards were right in opposing his marriage to Mary and in thinking he could not make her happy.

Abraham tormented himself with such thoughts as these until he decided the only fair thing to Mary was to ask her to release him from the engagement. It was on New Year's Day, 1841, that he went to the Edwards home with a heavy heart to tell her this. Afterwards he called this dreadful date "that fatal first" of January.

He possibly began by explaining that it was better to break the engagement because he could not support her in the way that would make her happy. Mary could recognize that this grew out of his unselfish concern for her. But she also knew her own mind. She was not afraid to face hard work and limited means as his wife. She showed her way of looking at it when she said on another occasion, "I would rather marry a good man — a man of mind — with a hope and bright prospects ahead for position — fame & power " than to marry all the "gold" in the world.

It was when the matter of that flirting scene came up that the girl gave way to her feelings. Her conscience had probably been hurting her anyway; it was one of her failings that she was always saying or doing something in quick anger and then deeply regretting it later. That flirting with Mr. Douglas as if he were the man she was most interested in had been a bit of deception to pay

Mr. Lincoln back for forgetting his date with her. When the subject was mentioned, she sprang up wringing her hands and burst into tears. She cried out brokenly, "the deceiver shall be deceived wo[e] is me."

Mr. Lincoln could not stand the sight of her distress. He took her tenderly in his arms and kissed away the tears. Then, torn by the conflict in his feelings, the distracted man fled from the house. It would be twenty-two months before he entered the Edwards home again. Fate would have to use her wits in strange ways to bring these two together once more.

Mary of course released him from the engagement as he had asked. Mr. Lincoln was almost frantic. He was probably unable to eat or sleep, for he fell ill. After a week in bed, he reappeared, looking very thin and pitiful. Caught between his love and longing for Mary and his feeling that he must stay away from her for her own good, he sank into the depths of depression. He kept away from all parties or occasions where he might meet the girl. Twenty-three days after the broken engagement he wrote his law partner, Mary's cousin John, "I am now the most miserable man living. If what I feel were equally distributed to the whole human family, there would not be one cheerful face on the earth."

In contrast to such complete misery there were those who were thoroughly delighted at the break between Mary and Mr. Lincoln. Mrs. Edwards thought it the best thing that could have happened and she was determined to prevent any renewal of the engagement. Mary's earnest beau Mr. Webb could not have been better pleased. He increased his visits and attentions so much that gossip soon had it that Mary would become Mrs. Webb.

The girl herself never once wavered in her love for Mr. Lincoln. At some time after the break between them, possibly when he was ill and so desperately "blue," she had the courage to write him that her feeling for him remained unchanged.

But in his distressed state of doubt and indecision, he continued to avoid all places where he might see her. This was easier to do because he had a sort of traveling law practice which took him out of town about half the time. He and other lawyers would go from town to town to hold court on what was called the judicial circuit. Mr. Lincoln was absent from Springfield about three months in the spring and three in the fall, though he could come back for an occasional weekend if he wanted to.

The long winter passed. With spring the level country around Springfield took on the bright colors of thousands of wildflowers. In June, Mary wrote to Merce, "Summer in all its beauty has again come, the prairie land looks as beautiful as it did in the olden time." "The olden time" to this young woman meant the year before, when she had had no heartache and loneliness.

She was keeping her chin up to the public but to Merce she confessed that she had a "sad spirit." "The last two or three months have been of *interminable* length," she wrote. This was in spite of the ardent attentions of Mr. Webb. The letter tells the outcome of this gentleman's wooing. He was not going to win Mary's hand in marriage. She was, as the old saying puts it, "giving him the mitten." "In your friendly & confiding ear," she wrote Merce, "allow me to whisper that my *heart can never be his*. I have deeply regretted that his constant visits, attentions &c should have given room for remarks, which were to me unpleasant." Mary perhaps feared that Mr. Lincoln would hear the gossip about Mr. Webb and herself and think she cared for the widower.

At last in her letter she shyly mentioned the man to whom she had been engaged. "I have not met *him* in the gay world for months," she confided to Mercy. "I would that the case were different, that he would once more resume his station in Society." If the saddened Mr. Lincoln could only feel like himself again, "much, much happiness would it afford me." So she too was sad and full of longing.

The "*interminable*" months continued to go by without change in the situation. The goldenrod of autumn came again to the prairie and then the snows of winter. As the spring of the year 1842 approached, Mr. Lincoln was much more like his old self. He had come to the conclusion that some of his doubts and forebodings had been, as he said, "all the worst sort of nonsense." At least he knew by this time that Mary gave no sign of marrying either Mr. Webb or Mr. Douglas. But he still did not know what was the right thing for him to do. And he was constantly haunted by the fear that Mary was now unhappy and that he was responsible for it. That thought, he wrote in March, "still kills my soul."

During this period when the two were estranged Mr. Lincoln's close friend, Joshua Speed, had fallen in love with a girl named Fanny Henning in Kentucky. The course of their true love was not running smoothly either. Mr. Lincoln wrote Joshua many letters of sympathetic advice with the result that Joshua's tangled emotions were straightened out and he married Fanny early in that year of 1842.

Abraham rejoiced over the happiness of his friend. He wrote Joshua, "I believe God made me one of the instruments of bringing your Fanny and you together, which union, I have no doubt He had fore-ordained." Mr. Lincoln had a deep faith in God and his divine guidance. He then told Joshua he was going to let God show him what was the right thing for him to do. Did God intend for him to stay away from Mary because he feared he could not make her happy, or was it "fore-ordained" that he should marry her in spite of poverty and family opposition. "Whatever he designs, he will do for *me* yet," wrote Abraham. " 'Stand *still* and see the salvation of the Lord' is my text just now."

To Mr. Lincoln "standing still" to see what God intended for him, there came a casual invitation to drop in at the home of his good friends, Mr. and Mrs. Simeon Francis, on a certain day and hour. Unaware of a warm-hearted little plot in which these two had become "instruments" also, he entered their home. Suddenly he found himself in a room with the girl who had haunted his thoughts for the last year and a half. Mary stood before him, her dear remembered face as surprised and tremulous as his own. Kind Mrs. Francis was telling them sympathetically to be friends again.

God had given Mr. Lincoln an unmistakable answer.

Mr. and Mrs. Francis had only to look at the telltale faces of Mary and Mr. Lincoln to know how they felt about each other. The Francises also knew that because of Mrs. Edwards's attitude the young lawyer could not go to the Edwards home to see Mary, so they offered their house as a place for the lovers to meet.

Now began a happy, exciting period of secret meetings that worked out like a bright, lively play on the stage. Mary, who loved both romance and drama, undoubtedly enjoyed every detail of the situation. In a day before telephones were even dreamed of, she and Mr. Lincoln must contrive to send notes or messages to each other to arrange the time. Great precautions must be taken to keep the Edwardses from finding out what was going on. Doubtless there were some narrow escapes from discovery to give added spice to the part Mary was playing.

Of course the engagement was renewed. The Francises, caring very much for these two young people who had suffered, were enjoying the romance taking place under their roof. One or two other intimate friends were in the secret and probably useful in quietly passing on a note or whispering an appointment to the tall lawyer or the bright-faced girl whom he was now calling "Molly" again. A small, gay, and sparkling group was often to be seen in the Francis parlor. Mary, her "sad spirit" completely gone, was radiant and vivacious. As for Mr. Lincoln, he did not even seem related to "the most miserable man living." The old twinkle had come back to his eyes and once more he was telling funny stories in that special droll way of his. Spirits ran high.

As it turned out, their spirits ran a little too high. The young lawyer was always in the thick of politics and so was Mr. Francis, who was editor of a Springfield newspaper. So there was much talk of local politics in general and in particular some joking about a rather pompous member of the Coterie, Mr. James Shields, who was a political opponent of Mr. Lincoln's. One witty or playful remark would lead to another and finally Mr. Lincoln wrote a funny letter ridiculing Mr. Shields. He signed the letter with an assumed name, "Rebecca," and Mr. Francis printed it in his newspaper.

You may have noticed that Mary often had impulsive ideas which she carried out without thinking of the consequences. People of course chuckled over Mr. Lincoln's comical letter signed "Rebecca." This was so much fun that Mary and a girl friend of hers concocted another letter signed "Rebecca," which put Mr. Shields in a very ridiculous light. Mr. Francis printed this letter in his paper too. Mary then wrote some clever verses along the same line and they also were printed.

No one had stopped to consider that Mr. Shields was a hotheaded man who had been trained in dueling back in Ireland, where he came from. Strange as it seems, a few scattered duels were still being fought at this time. Mr. Shields furiously demanded of Editor Francis the real name of the one who had written those three pieces belittling him. Mr. Francis consulted Mr. Lincoln, who said he would take the responsibility for the two Mary had written as well as for the one which was his own. Mr. Shields promptly challenged Mr. Lincoln to a duel. The bright, sweet course of the romance was suddenly darkened with the threat of bloodshed and tragedy.

Mr. Lincoln hated the cruel and unjust practice of dueling, but if he declined to fight he would be called a coward and "no gentleman." He accepted the challenge and the time for the duel was set. For several days elaborate preparations were going forward for the meeting on Bloody Island, which was quite a distance away in the Mississippi River. Springfield was almost beside itself with excitement.

It is not hard to imagine the turmoil of Mary's feelings in the period of waiting, her worried days and sleepless nights. Mr. Lincoln might be killed. A friend of her father's had been killed in a duel not long before she left Kentucky. Mr. Shields had been trained in swordsmanship, but what did her dear, awkward Mr. Lincoln know about that nimble and deadly art? The duel was partly her fault, as he had taken the blame for what she had written.

She was proud of the way he was acting, though that only increased her love and anxiety. The situation seemed like something out of a novel of the age of chivalry, when a gallant knight would go forth to battle for the lady of his choice. Mr. Lincoln was her gallant knight; he was ready to fight for her. She called him "my champion."

On the appointed day the two duelists with their long swords, their doctors, their "seconds," and a few other friends repaired by horse and boat to the dueling place on Bloody Island. All had set, grim faces. But some of these good friends had level heads and they went into action to prevent the duel. Arguing with the hotheaded Mr. Shields was anything but easy, but finally a reconciliation was arranged and the duel was called off.

Living through this harrowing experience, with its intensity of excitement, fear, and then enormous relief, had brought the engaged couple closer together than ever. A marriage was now being planned at these precious stolen meetings at the Francis home. Because of Mrs. Edwards's opposition any wedding festivities seemed out of the question. They would simply go to the minister's home and have him marry them without ado.

The date was set, November 4, 1842. Mr. Lincoln

bought a wedding ring and in it he had the jeweler en-
grave three words which expressed the sacredness of
this marriage to them both: *Love is Eternal.*

Mrs. Edwards knew nothing of the renewed engagement and these preparations. Mary and Mr. Lincoln decided it was best to complete all their arrangements first
and not tell her until the very morning of their wedding
day. Both suspected there was going to be an awful row
when she heard the news.

"To Love and to Cherish"

ᴇᴀʀʟʏ on that Friday morning of November 4, Mary told her sister Elizabeth that she was going to marry Mr. Lincoln that day. Elizabeth, her face outraged, broke into a storm of protest. How could she let her headstrong younger sister marry this roughhewn man from the backwoods, this plebeian? Didn't Mary have any family pride? "Do not forget that you are a Todd," cried Elizabeth furiously. Why did the girl have to choose that gawky Abraham Lincoln, a man plainly from the lower classes, when she had suitable beaux like Mr. Webb and Mr. Douglas? Elizabeth poured out her scathing comments with flashing eyes.

Mary could be counted on to give back words as stinging as those she received. Her eyes too flashed fire as the quarrel raged. She did not yield an inch. No matter what Elizabeth said or thought, Mr. Lincoln was the man she loved and believed in and she was going to marry him that day. And neither Elizabeth nor anyone else was going to stop her.

Meanwhile the prospective bridegroom had met Mr Ninian Edwards on the street and told him the news. Mr. Edwards came home to find the two sisters still making quite a scene. He had come to the sensible conclusion that since he and his wife could not prevent the marriage, they might as well make the best of it. He felt that as Mary was his ward, it would look a lot better and cause less talk in the town if the wedding took place in the Edwards home with a few invited guests.

Elizabeth listened to her husband and she recognized the truth of what he said. But she broke out in fresh lamentations. Like all the Todd women, she knew how to be a gracious hostess and she took pride in the elaborateness and perfection of her parties. How could she ever get ready to entertain guests that evening with the day already half gone? There was no skillful Monsieur Giron in Springfield to whom she could send a note requesting an emergency wedding cake. The only bakery in town was Dickey's and the best he could offer was gingerbread and beer. Elizabeth needled her sister by saying, "I guess I will have to send to old Dickey's for some of his gingerbread and beer." Mary, still smarting over the terms applied to Mr. Lincoln, replied hotly, "Well, that will be good enough for plebeians, I suppose."

Elizabeth knew that wedding cake would have to be baked in her own kitchen. She doubtless looked up the recipe with the rebellious expression of a woman who has had about all she can take.

A messenger was hurriedly sent to the third sister, Frances Wallace, asking her to come quickly to help with the preparations. The Todd family was a loyal clan and all the kinsfolk rallied round in this emergency. The gentlemen relayed invitations to various close friends while the ladies went into feverish activity in the Edwards kitchen. Footsteps hurried to and fro assembling eggs, butter, and sugar and soon came the pleasant sound of someone vigorously beating the rich batter. By and by the smell of a cake baking indicated the ladies were winning in their race against time.

Meanwhile Mary was too busy and excited for words. She was going to have a wedding party after all! She must ask some of her friends to be bridesmaids.

Her cousin Elizabeth Todd, daughter of Dr. John Todd, her uncle, looking out of the window of her home, was surprised to see Mary running down the street with the air of one who has important news. Entering breathlessly, the girl exclaimed, "Oh Elizabeth, I'm going to be married tonight to Mr. Lincoln and I want you to stand up with me!" Elizabeth's first thought was a very feminine one, "I've nothing to wear." Mary said immediately, "You must get something." After consulting together, the two decided that Elizabeth's best white dress would do if she washed and ironed it. Mary doubtless left her getting out the washtub.

Mary herself had to make her own best party dress

serve as a wedding gown. It is not possible to know exactly what it was like, but a girl who so loved clothes could be counted on to have something pretty and stylish. The fashion of the time called for a closely fitted bodice, a pinched-in waist and, flaring out from this tiny waist, the glory of a wide, full hoop skirt. Low necks were stylish too and Mary could take advantage of that fact to reveal her pretty white throat and shoulders.

That evening carriages were climbing the hill to the Edwards home. All was in readiness for them. Those hurrying hands and feet in the kitchen had triumphed: a handsome wedding cake stood waiting to be served. The timing, however, had been very close and the cake was still warm from the baking! A tablecloth with a turtledove design, which was thought to be very appropriate for weddings, covered the dining table.

The minister took his place in front of the mantel, the light from its two oil lamps falling upon his open prayer book. The assembled guests, about thirty in all, saw only the backs of the couple that stood before him, the tall man with the dark shaggy hair and the dainty girl who looked so amusingly short beside him.

In the hush that fell rain could be heard beating against the windowpanes. The clergyman began the beautiful words of the marriage service. He placed the girl's small white hand in Mr. Lincoln's brown and powerful fist. With her bright head uplifted she repeated after the minister in a soft, tremulous voice, "I Mary take thee

Abraham to my wedded Husband, to have and to hold from this day forward, for better for worse, for richer for poorer, in sickness and in health, to love and to cherish, till death us do part."

Afterwards there were congratulations, merriment of friends, and the cutting of that wedding cake. It seemed strange to Mary to hear people calling her "Mrs. Lincoln." Most brides are nervous, especially when they are getting married under family disapproval. It is no wonder she spilled coffee on her dress.

They were not to have a honeymoon journey; such trips took too much time and money. After the festivities Mary and her husband went out from that rich scene of gaiety to proceed through the rain to the room he had engaged in a simple boardinghouse. The married life of Mr. and Mrs. Abraham Lincoln had begun.

Fate had at last joined the lives of Mary and Abraham into one line. That line of their futures would rise and fall; it would have peaks of happiness and success and depressions of disappointment and sorrow. All the while the line would be slowly rising until suddenly it would shoot up to a dizzy height. But in whatever life brought to them these two would keep the vows they had taken that night: they would love and cherish each other as long as they lived.

· 8 ·

"We Have Another Boy"

*T*HE winter went by with its usual snows and freezes. Spring brought thawing and then again the prairie was colored with its wildflowers. In May, Mr. Lincoln wrote his friend Joshua Speed, "We are not keeping house, but boarding at the Globe Tavern," adding that their room and board cost only four dollars a week. Surely even a poor lawyer could afford that much.

Living at a tavern was a new experience for Mary. Often as she sat sewing in their room she would hear the ringing of the big bell on the roof when a stagecoach drove up in front. Its clanging would be followed by the rapid footsteps of the stablemen, running to take charge of the horses. With her natural interest in people Mary would want to know who had arrived. With so much going and coming the Globe Tavern was an interesting place to live.

But inevitably she missed the handsome furnishings and beauty of the Edwards home. She must also have missed the lovely grove of trees around it. The Globe

Tavern was near the center of town, about a block and a half from the public square where the state capitol stood. Mary's view was a bare one, a few small-town stores perhaps, and a roadway which was sometimes almost knee-deep in mud and sometimes almost as deep in dust.

Surroundings, however, did not matter too much in those first months together. She could watch or listen for Mr. Lincoln's footsteps when he came home from his law office, and his eyes would light up when he saw her face. They could sit together in the evenings and each could tell the other what had happened since morning. Mary was interested in all the details of her husband's day, and this was a sweet, new experience to a man who had known much loneliness.

They could make their plans for the future. They were not going to live in a boardinghouse always; Mary was sure her husband was going to be wonderfully successful. She was good at sizing people up and she had recognized that Mr. Lincoln had unusual qualities of mind and heart. He could take a tangled public question, look at it from all sides, think it out, and then put it in such clear, simple words that anyone could understand it. She believed confidently he was going to be an important man some day. He lacked confidence in himself and was sometimes "blue," so her optimism was good medicine for him.

February 12 was his birthday and Mary planned a small celebration of the day in that first year. She made a happy little speech to him which ended, "I am so glad you have a birthday. I feel so grateful to your mother." How his eyes must have softened as he listened to her! It is extremely doubtful that he had had any celebration of his birthday before. His early life had been too much a matter of bare necessities for living.

By spring they were talking about something very dear to them both, the fact that they were going to have a baby. The sewing in which Mary was now engaged was baby dresses, dresses about twice as long as any baby could possibly be, for it was the style then for babies, like their mothers, to wear very lengthy clothes. Few people have had a greater love for children than Mary and Mr. Lincoln, and the prospect of having a child of their own meant everything to them.

Their tender planning together for this coming event was interrupted in April, when Mr. Lincoln had to start out, as usual, on his rounds of the judicial circuit. This traveling law practice kept him away from Springfield most of April and May that spring, with only an occasional weekend trip back home. Mary learned for the first time how hard this necessary absence of her husband was going to be in her married life. She had so quickly become accustomed to his loved and comforting presence, which brought her contentment, that she was becoming dependent on him. She missed him terribly and a friend who was on the circuit with him wrote back to Springfield that Mr. Lincoln was "desperately homesick."

Mary's husband, however, was most assuredly in Springfield that day in August when word passed around among those in the Globe Tavern that the Lincoln baby was arriving. Many strange sounds had been heard within the tavern in its time but none more strange or moving than the little brassy cry of a newborn infant that rang out in the Lincolns' room that day. Later Mary remembered, she wrote, how "my darling husband, was bending over me, with such love and tenderness — when . . . that babe — was born."

The child was a boy. No couple could have felt more deeply the joy and fulfillment of parenthood. Two heads bent over this miracle of their own baby, Mr. Lincoln's eyes lighted with happiness and pride and Mary's face transfigured with mother love. From this time on the nickname "Molly," which Mr. Lincoln had used in courtship days, disappeared. Sometimes he would call Mary by playful pet names like "Puss," "child-wife," or "little woman," but mostly after this he called her "Mother."

They named their son Robert Todd Lincoln after Mary's father. Before long Mr. Todd made the tedious trip from Lexington to Springfield to see his new grandson and namesake, meet Mary's husband, and visit all three of his married daughters living in Springfield. How Mary's face must have shone when she presented her son to the father she loved. "May God bless and protect my little namesake," he said with deep feeling.

With wifely pride she also introduced to him her tall

The Lincoln Home on Eighth Street

In the upper picture Mr. Lincoln stands behind the fence with Willie. They are also in the lower right picture, with the addition of Tad, who has climbed up on the fence. At the lower left is the back yard, with the pump near the back door from which water must be carried into the kitchen.

husband. Mr. Todd recognized that Mary had married a good and trustworthy man and he was ready to help the little family of three. He made arrangements on this trip to advance a certain amount of money to Mary until Mr. Lincoln was more firmly established in his law practice. It was not a large amount but it helped a lot. The Todd relatives were all accepting the marriage now and the Lincolns were included in family dinners and parties. But Mrs. Edwards and others of the clan kept on regarding Mr. Lincoln as somewhat inferior, a fact that irritated Mary a great deal and put her on the defensive.

The Lincolns called their little son Bob or Bobbie. The Globe Tavern was not proving a good place for a baby. Apparently Bobbie objected to being awakened by the big bell or the noise of the other boarders and raised his voice in such vigorous protest that the other boarders in their turn objected to being kept awake by him! It is a safe guess that if any one of them made a slighting remark about this in Mary's hearing, that person would get a quick and untactful retort. Mary was not one to take criticism kindly, especially criticism of her wonderful child.

The Lincolns, however, began that fall to look for another abiding place. They found a tiny three-room frame cottage on South Fourth Street and moved there. The details of their months in this house are not known. They soon considered it only a temporary place to live. Out on Eighth Street at the corner where Jackson Street crossed it was a story-and-a-half cottage belonging to

Dr. Dresser, the minister who had married them. There was a chance that he would sell it and the Lincolns were eying it with great interest. You can picture them walking slowly past it one day, perhaps in December, the tall man and the short wife, one of them carrying the well-wrapped-up baby, both looking with longing at the house and planning what they would do with it if it became their home. There was a back yard which would be so nice for Bobbie to play in when he grew bigger. And they certainly ought to have a home of their own, now that they had started their family. They could afford it if they economized in other things. The decision was made and in January lawyer Lincoln drew up the contract to buy the house from Dr. Dresser.

They had to wait four months before they could get possession of the house. It was May and the prairie wildflowers were again coming into bloom when they moved in. Mary must now set up housekeeping in earnest, and it was an age when household tasks had to be done in a way that now seems terribly laborious.

She must be responsible for three meals a day for her little family. She must cook them on an iron stove with a wood fire. Firewood does not grow in kitchens; it must be chopped in the back yard and carried in by armfuls. At bedtime the kitchen fire must be banked — heaped up and covered with ashes — so that it would burn very low but not go out during the night. If it did go out, the mistress of the house, entering her kitchen on a cold morning to prepare breakfast, had to get some kindling wood and start a new one. This was not a simple matter. Matches had been invented by the time Mary was married but they were not the satisfactory matches of today, they cost money, and people clung to the old way of borrowing fire from a friend. Mr. Lincoln, carrying a shovel, would cross the street to a neighbor's and ask if he might have a live coal. Sometimes by the time the fire had been lighted and had become hot enough to cook anything, Mary may have felt she had done half a morning's work. It was a far thing from cooking with gas or electricity.

There was no running water in Mary's kitchen — it had to be carried in buckets from the pump that stood in the back yard near the kitchen door. (Inconvenient as that was, it may have seemed quite a luxury to Mr. Lincoln when he remembered how he, as a boy, had had to carry water from a spring that was a mile away from his father's cabin.) It took lots of water for cooking and washing clothes, dishes, and themselves in this new home on Eighth Street. As with all babies, Bobbie had special washing to be done every day.

Mary and other housewives were used to these primitive ways of doing things. They had not known anything else. But growing up in Lexington with many house servants, Mary had not had to do these things herself. There had been no chance to learn to cook. Dear, cross Aunt Chaney had not encouraged the Todd "chil'en" to mess around in her kitchen. The thought of Aunt Chaney and Old Nelson and their loyal, experienced service must have brought many a pang of longing to Mary in those early days of her housekeeping. Servants were few and very hard to get (and keep) in Springfield and the Lincolns at this time could not afford to pay high wages. Mary did have a girl to help her off and on, but as Aunt Chaney back home, hearing reports, said, they "didn't even know how to make good co'n bread." Aunt Chaney lamented the fact that way out in Illinois "Miss Mary didn't have no beaten biscuits at home." But such biscuits were not for the over-busy young housewife, they required know-how and a great deal of strong-arm beating of the dough. People would know they were to have beaten biscuits for breakfast when they heard resounding whacks from the kitchen.

Mary did have to make bread for her family; the loaves could not be bought at a store as now. She must knead the great mass of dough on the kitchen table, place it in a bowl, and set it in a warm place to rise. Sometimes it did not rise enough and the bread was heavy. Sometimes, if forgotten, it rose too much and ran over the edge of the bowl. There was the added hazard of keeping the fire just right, so that the bread would bake thoroughly without burning.

Mary found these unaccustomed tasks hard. But she was a young woman who had much courage and cheerfulness and was not afraid of hard work. She was a bit proud of her small white hands, whose quick little gestures were a part of her personality, but she did not hold those hands back from any work necessary for her family. In time her hands lost their softness.

She cooked and washed. She tended the baby. She filled the oil lamps, trimmed their wicks, and polished their glass chimneys. She wiped up the black Illinois mud tracked in from Springfield's unpaved streets. She even, in those early days of her homemaking, made her own soap, pouring water over wood ashes to get lye to combine with the grease she had saved.

She did not enjoy drudgery, of course, but she delighted in making her home pretty and attractive. Her housewifely instinct took great satisfaction in selecting a new chair or sofa, in making curtains and draperies for her windows, and in acquiring lovely dishes. By and by when Mr. Lincoln became more prominent and made more money, as he was sure to do, they would need these things for entertaining. She was the kind of homemaker to whom each bright new object for her home gave a thrill.

Mary was a happy wife in the cottage on Eighth Street. When evening came she was apt to stop her work frequently to look out of the window toward town. She was watching for her husband to come home to supper. When finally she spied the tall figure wearing a tall hat (as all the lawyers did), she would run to meet him at their gate. There she would slip her hand in his, and swinging their hands together they would walk to the front door and enter.

In that small domain of home the baby, Bobbie, was

now undoubtedly reigning as king. No woman ever enjoyed her motherhood more than Mary. To care for her baby, to nurse him, dress him and hold him in her arms gave her supreme happiness. Mr. Lincoln was an equally doting parent. After supper, perhaps, he would lie down in their hall, his shoulders on a turned-down chair, his feet up on the post at the foot of the stairs, and dangle the baby over him in happy play.

Parental joy goes along with parental anxieties and fears. Soon Bobbie was not wearing the long infant gowns any more, and almost before they knew it he had his second birthday. He was a bright, quick, active little fellow and after he learned to toddle around he was into everything. Mary had too much to do to watch him every minute and one day an accident occurred which frightened her terribly.

It came about through another primitive living arrangement, the wooden privy which stood in the back yard. The Lincoln home, like those around it, had no inside toilet. In summer the privy was a smelly place and quicklime was sprinkled around to keep down the odor and to make it as clean as they could. A box of lime was kept at hand for this purpose and one day Bobbie got to this box and put some of the lime in his mouth. Mary knew the lime was a powerful poison and, always excitable, she went into a panic at this threat to her child. Mr. Lincoln was not at home and she screamed to her neighbors for help, crying out frantically, "Bobbie will die! Bobbie will die!" A friend from across the street rushed to the rescue and washed out the boy's mouth.

When Bobbie was in his third year, Mary brought out the long baby dresses again and freshened them up. She was expecting another child early that spring. It was the second week in March when she knew the time had come to send for the doctor, who was probably Dr. William Wallace, her own brother-in-law, the husband of her sister Frances. Somewhat later Mr. Lincoln wrote the news to his friend Joshua Speed, "We have another boy, born the 10th of March," adding, "He is very much such a child as Bob was at his age — rather of a longer order." Then the father gave a neat description of his firstborn: "Bob is 'short and low,' and I expect, always will be. He talks very plainly — almost as plainly as anybody. He is quite smart enough. . . . He has a great deal of that sort of mischief that is the offspring of much animal spirits." The last sentence is a polite, roundabout way of saying that Bob was very rambunctious and sometimes more than his mother could manage.

As if to furnish proof of this, while Mr. Lincoln was still engaged in writing this letter at his office, someone arrived to tell him that Bobbie had run off and could not be found. The father at once left his desk and went home. By the time he arrived there Bobbie had been located and brought back, so Mr. Lincoln returned to the law office to finish his letter. He told Joshua Speed about the interruption and remarked, out of his experience with his headstrong little son, "and by now, very likely he is run away again."

It is possible that Bob resented the fact that his new little brother was getting so much attention. Before this second baby came, he had been the center of everything. Now he had to share the rule of his little kingdom with another. But no matter how Bob felt about the new baby, Mary and her husband welcomed him with open arms. They named him Edward Baker Lincoln after a dear friend and began calling him little Eddie.

Eddie's arrival was a happy event for his parents. Another thrilling event was to happen to them that same year of 1846, something they both wanted very, very much. Mr. Lincoln had been working hard and growing more prominent in Springfield since his marriage, but he wanted to achieve more than local prominence. It was said of him that "His ambition was a little engine that knew no rest." Mary had her own little engine of ambition that ran along with his and sometimes got ahead of it. The two loved to plan for the bright future together.

He had been in the state legislature of Illinois for several terms, and now he wanted an office that would take him into affairs that concerned the whole country. What he and Mary had been hoping for quite a while was that he would be elected to the United States House of Representatives.

They had had setbacks and disappointments, as everyone is apt to have in the game of politics. Mr. Lincoln would sometimes get discouraged and then he needed Mary's faith in him to restore his confidence. But not ong after Eddie's birth the couple got their wish. Mr. Lincoln was elected to Congress. The next year he was to go to Washington to become a member of the House of Representatives in the nation's capital.

There was joy and excitement in the cottage on Eighth Street. Mary's spirit soared. She had been right all along about Mr. Lincoln being a rising man, and she just knew he would rise higher yet.

The Lincolns gave a party at their house. It was probably Mary's idea that a congressman-elect should entertain his friends. One of the guests was a young man named Ward Lamon whom Mr. Lincoln had met not long before. Mr. Lamon remarked to Mary that her husband was a great favorite in the eastern part of Illinois, where he, Mr. Lamon, had been staying recently. The young wife's face beamed with pride and pleasure. "Yes," she replied, "he is a great favorite everywhere." Then she added gaily, "He is to be President of the United States some day."

It is a safe guess that she was the only one in Springfield who thought so. Certainly Mr. Lincoln himself did not and most emphatically none of her relatives did. They would have said the very idea was ridiculous.

· 9 ·

"I Hate to Stay in This Old Room by Myself"

*I*N the fall of 1847 Mary was busy with thrilling plans. She and the children were going to Washington with Mr. Lincoln. Neither she nor her husband had ever been to the famous capital of their country and they looked forward to it eagerly. They would see historic places like the White House and the Capitol where the great statesmen of the nation had walked and lived.

The little family would stop on their way at Lexington, Kentucky, and visit Mary's old home. Her stepmother would welcome them kindly for a visit now that Mary was off her hands. It would mean so much to see her loved father and find out how much the half brothers and half sisters had grown since she left home eight years ago. How would little Emilie, who had been a beautiful three-year-old girl when last Mary saw her, look now? What joy it would be to introduce her tall husband (about to enter the House of Representatives, you know) to all the relatives and friends and esspecially to Mr. Henry Clay, who was the idol of them both.

How she had to hustle around to get ready! The house must be rented while they were away and all the furniture stored in "the North up-stairs room." She must pack the trunk or trunks and what a task it was. How would you go about folding the yards and yards of a hoop skirt, not to mention packing the extra hoops themselves? She must think out all the things the children would need on the long, slow journey.

Before Mary and her husband left they had a strange new experience. A Frenchman named Daguerre had recently invented a way of "taking pictures," as it was called. Mary was used to painted portraits — her father sat for a splendid one — but this was different. You could sit in front of an apparatus, staying very still for a few minutes, and later you would get a little likeness of yourself several inches high. People, filled with wonder, were talking about this new invention, saying who ever heard of such a thing and what will they invent next. Now a man had come to Springfield who could take these daguerreotypes, as the pictures were called.

It was probably Mary who decided that Congressman-elect Lincoln and his wife ought to have their pictures taken. When the day and hour for the sitting arrived, she put on a lovely striped dress and fastened it at the throat with a large cameo pin. Over this she wore a lace scarf, the whole effect being very satisfactory. Carefully she parted her bright brown hair on the side, brush-

The picture of Mr. Lincoln by courtesy of the Library of Congress; the one of Mrs.
Lincoln through the kindness of William H. Townsend

The Lincolns Try the
New Invention

About the time Mr. Lincoln was elected to Congress, people in Springfield were talking about a wonderful new machine which took pictures. Dressed in their best, Mary and Mr. Lincoln sit for their first photographs.

ing it to a glossy smoothness in front but letting it fall in little curls behind her ears. When Mr. Lincoln had put on his best suit she must have brushed his unruly hair too, for it was to look unusually tidy in the picture.

The photographer doubtless put a clamp back of Mary's head to keep her from moving. Posing rigidly for several minutes was a nervous business and usually resulted in a somewhat frozen expression. Mary later said that her pictures all made her look too stern and her hands too large. The last, of course, was because her hands were nearer the camera.

The pictures of Mr. and Mrs. Lincoln hung together in the Lincoln home on Eighth Street for many years. Bob, when he was grown, said he could not remember when they were not there. It is a wonderful thing that today you can gaze on these pictures and see the young couple as they looked when they started on their long journey east with their two children.

They followed the same route Mary had traveled when she came to Springfield, going by stagecoach to St. Louis, then down the Mississippi River by steamboat, and next up the Ohio and Kentucky Rivers. More than a week had passed by the time they reached Frankfort and there at last Mary spied the familiar little train, "the Nottaway," standing on the narrow track. She and Mr. Lincoln bundled their two children aboard its single coach. How beautiful the Kentucky landscape, even in early November, must have looked to her homecoming eyes. By and by the outskirts of Lexington appeared and then suddenly they were rattling along familiar Water Street and then into the neat little railroad depot, looking exactly as it had when she left on that October day eight years before. Oh, it was good to see the Todd carriage waiting!

They were soon driven the short distance to the stately home on Main Street. The front door was thrown open to receive them. In the wide hall the whole Todd family stood to welcome them, Mary's fine-looking father, her stepmother and a whole flock of assorted half brothers and sisters. Standing out prettily among them were three little girls wearing crimson merino dresses, white kid boots, and ruffled white muslin aprons. One of the small crimson figures was Emilie, now about eleven years old.

Emilie's eyes were fixed on that open doorway with intense interest. She perhaps could not recall her half sister who had left when she was three, but she always remembered vividly how Mary looked as she entered, carrying little Eddie in her arms and with her face glowing with the joy of this homecoming. "To my mind," said Emilie later, "she was lovely, clear, sparkling, blue eyes, lovely smooth white skin with a fresh, faint wild-rose color in her cheeks; and glossy light brown hair, which fell in soft, short curls behind each ear." The words paint the face in the daguerreotype in living color.

Mr. Lincoln followed his wife carrying Bobbie. He stooped to put the little fellow on the floor, said Emilie, "and as he arose I remember thinking of Jack and the Beanstalk, and feared he might be the hungry giant of the story, he was so tall and looked so big with a long full black cloak over his shoulders and he wore a fur cap with ear straps which allowed but little of his face to be seen." Emilie almost expected him to start saying, "Fee, fi, fo, fum!" in true giant fashion. Half shy, half frightened, she hid behind her mother's hoop skirts, an ample hiding place.

Mary was kissing and embracing all the family with joyous exclamations of greeting and wonder at the way the children had grown and changed. At the back of the hall stood Mammy Sally and the other servants, their dark faces beaming with welcome. Mary flew to greet them too and to show them her two boys. What a comfort it was to put little Eddie in Mammy's experienced arms. Here was someone with whom she could really trust her baby. The servants all made much ado over "Miss Mary's chil'en."

Meanwhile Mr. Lincoln had been shaking hands with Mr. and Mrs. Todd and meeting the various young people. He had not failed to notice Emilie's shy retreat behind her mother's skirts, so presently he reached down and lifted Emilie in his arms saying, "So this is little sister." Her fear vanished; suddenly she felt very safe in those strong, gentle arms. Always afterward Mr. Lincoln called her "Little Sister," and he and Mary loved her especially.

Something very funny had happened just before the

Lincolns entered the Todd hall. Unknown to them Mrs. Todd's nephew, Joseph Humphreys, had traveled on the same railway coach with them from Frankfort. By now you have probably guessed that such doting parents as Mary and Mr. Lincoln did not restrain their children very much. Joseph Humphreys evidently had the same strict ideas about child-raising as his aunt, Mary's step-mother. He reached the Todd home ahead of the Lincolns and, after greetings, he burst out: "Aunt Betsy, I was never so glad to get off a train in my life. There were two lively youngsters on board who kept the whole train in a turmoil, and their long-legged father, instead of spanking the brats, looked pleased as Punch and aided and abetted the older one in mischief."

At this point he happened to glance out of the window and saw that the Todd carriage had stopped in front of the house. The "long-legged" man got out of it and turned to lift out the "two lively youngsters." "Good Lord," exclaimed Joseph, "there they are now." He promptly vanished through another door and stayed away the whole time the Lincolns were in town!

Mary had a wonderful three weeks' visit, seeing relatives and old friends. It was good to enjoy leisurely living once more and be waited on by the loved household servants. It was like old times to sit again at the long dining table with all the children and grown-ups around it and to enter into the family fun and teasing. Mary's half brother Sam delighted in teaching Bobbie to call him "Uncle Sam," and took a fling at Mary for being so short by remarking, "I hope my nephews will inherit their father's long legs." "And their mother's lovely disposition," returned Mary, making a little face. She knew her own failing, that she was a bit peppery and sometimes said things she was sorry for later.

It was late in November when the Lincolns said good-by to all the Todds and started on the week-long journey to Washington. Soon after they arrived they settled in a pleasant boardinghouse just opposite the Capitol. Then began some months of eager new experiences for Mary and her husband.

The big dining room of the boardinghouse looked out over Capitol Park, as people then called the grounds around the Capitol. Capitol Park was filled with lovely trees and shrubs. The iron railing which enclosed it at that time was within fifty feet of their front door. Often on Saturday evenings there would be a band concert in the park and the Lincolns enjoyed walking over to mingle with the gay crowd and listen to the music. Perhaps Mr. Lincoln carried Eddie while Mary held Bobbie firmly by the hand.

When Congressman Lincoln could get away from his work they certainly visited some of Washington's historic places. It is pleasant to picture their first glimpse of the White House and imagine Mary saying buoyantly, "Maybe we'll live there some day," and Mr. Lincoln giving her an indulgent smile as his answer.

But most of the time he was busy with his duties in the House of Representatives and she had her hands full with the active Bobbie and with Eddie, who was at the stage of getting into everything. It was the old story that a boardinghouse is no place for babies and young children. By spring it was decided that Mary should take the boys and return to Lexington for another visit while Mr. Lincoln finished his term in Congress.

During the time they were thus separated the devoted couple wrote each other as often as they could. By good fortune several of these letters have been preserved. Reading them is like hearing Mary and Mr. Lincoln talk together. It is as if the faces in those daguerreotypes suddenly come to life, turn, and begin to speak to each other.

His first letter was written on a Sunday in April and he began by telling her how much he missed her. Since she had left he had had nothing but business to fill his days and he found it "exceedingly tasteless." Looking around the empty room which had been so gay and cozy when they had been in it together, he wrote, "I hate to stay in this old room by myself."

Mr. Lincoln not only missed his wife, he worried about her. He mentioned in this letter a trouble Mary had which caused her much suffering and greatly affected her life. She was one of those unlucky persons who have migraine headaches, a malady that comes especially to intense and sensitive people. These headaches came at frequent intervals and made her so ill and miserable that she could not lift her head from the pillow and even a jarring step on the floor was agony to her. Strain such as too much housework and constant care of the children tended to increase them. These illnesses were a constant problem to the Lincolns.

At Lexington, where she was free from housekeeping and could get help with the boys, she was finding herself better in this respect and had told him this good news in a letter. He was so glad about it. "Are you entirely free from headache?" he wrote. "That is good — good considering it is the first spring you have been free from it since we were acquainted." He was so happy about it that he added a playful and loving bit of nonsense: "I am afraid you will get so well, and fat, and young, as to be wanting to marry again. . . . Get weighed and write me how much you weigh." In another letter he urged her to get a girl as nurse to take charge of the little boys.

The leading topic of conversation in these letters was, of course, their wonderful children. Mary had written asking him to buy some "little plaid stockings" for Eddie's "dear little feet." He reported dutifully that he had gone to two stores without finding the kind she had described but he would try again tomorrow. What did Bobbie and Eddie "think of the little letters father sent them? Don't let the blessed fellows forget father," he wrote.

On a warm evening in May, Mary sat down in her room at the Todd home in Lexington to write to "My Dear Husband." Outside her window the lilac hedge was in bloom in the lovely garden where she and Elizabeth Humphreys had once hunted for a little lost turkey who turned out to be a mockingbird. It was *"Saturday night,"* she wrote him and "our babies are asleep." She must tell him about the boys. "Do not fear the children, have forgotten you," she said, adding that even little Eddie's eyes "brighten at the mention of your name." Their Eddie was now two years old. He had had a "little spell of sickness," his mother wrote, but he was all right again.

She must tell him a story about Eddie, especially since Mr. Lincoln was so fond of cats. Bobbie had brought a stray kitten to the house and as soon as Eddie spied it, "his *tenderness* broke forth, he made them bring it *water*" and fed it himself "with his *own dear hands*. He was a delighted little creature over it."

It happened that Mary's stepmother was one of those people who hate cats. While Eddie was happily caring for the kitten, Mary wrote, her stepmother came in and "in a very unfeeling manner, she ordered the servant near, to throw it out, which of *course*, was done, Ed. screaming & protesting loudly against the proceeding, *she* never appeared to mind his screams, which were long & loud, I assure you." Eddie was outraged. Stray animals were not treated that way at his home in Springfield; they were taken in, fed, cared for, petted and loved.

Since the subject had come up, Mary told Mr. Lincoln that her stepmother was treating her nicely. "She is very obliging & accommodating," Mary wrote, "but if she thought any of us, were on her hands again, I believe she would be *worse* than ever. . . . By the way," continued Mary, "she has just sent me up a glass of ice cream, for which this warm evening, I am duly grateful."

Mr. Lincoln had told Mary in his letter how much he missed her, how desolate the room which had been theirs together now seemed without her presence. In her letter to him from her lovely room at Lexington, she expressed the same longing: "How much, I wish instead of writing, we were together this evening, I feel very sad away from you."

· I O ·

Three Dark Events
and Two Bright Ones

ᴇARLY in October 1848 a newspaper in Springfield announced that "Hon. A. Lincoln and Family" were returning home. Mary, going from Lexington, had apparently joined her husband at some point on the trip. Since their house was rented they stayed at the Globe Tavern, so full of memories for them both.

When Mr. Lincoln had to return to Washington in November he left his family at the tavern. He would not be back until the following spring and he knew his wife was terribly afraid when she was in the house alone with the children.

Like many people Mary was very brave about some things and very timid about others. She faced hard tasks and difficulties with pluck and cheerfulness and she did not "baby" herself when she was ill or in pain. But she seems to have grown up with a feeling of insecurity and this feeling would pop to the surface under certain conditions.

For instance, there had been the day when an old umbrella-mender came to the door of the Lincoln home. He was harmless but he wore a ragged beard and something in his appearance and manner frightened Mary. She went into one of her panics, screaming to the neighbors to come help her. She had not learned, at the first warning surge of panic, to clamp on the brakes of self-control. It was a weakness of hers that she gave way too quickly to her feelings.

She was afraid of thunderstorms. Perhaps, as with a number of persons, she had once been stunned by lightning which struck very close to her. Mr. Lincoln knew of this agonizing terror and, at the first ominous rumble of approaching storm, he would leave his desk at the law office and walk quickly home to comfort her. Mary, nervous but confident that he would come, would be watching for him and would meet him at their little gate. He would put his protecting arm around her and so they would enter the house together.

Her husband's very protectiveness made it harder for Mary when he was away from home. Responsibility weighed upon her and she wanted to have some person calmer and more self-controlled than she was to whom she could turn in an emergency. When she was alone with the children and darkness settled down over the unlighted streets outside the cottage, while inside the lamps threw long black shadows, she was in an agony of fear. The children looked to her to watch over them and take care of them and she could not trust herself not to go into a panic. And what was she to do when her head-aches came and she was too ill to lift her head from the pillow?

It was the great hardship of her married life that Mr. Lincoln had to be away on the judicial circuit about three months in the spring and three in the fall. He came home at weekends when he could, but travel by stagecoach, steamboat, or horse and buggy was so slow that often he could not make the trip. He did the best he could to ease those nights of trembling fear for Mary. He paid a half-grown neighbor boy to sleep at the house while he was away. But no young boy could give her a sense of security.

It was a good arrangement then for the little family to stay at the Globe Tavern while Congressman Lincoln went back to Washington to finish his term. The long winter went by with its milestones of Christmas, New Year's, and "father's" birthday. Mary's heart was full of gladness when on the last day of March her husband came home again. The little family was united and set-tled once more in the cottage on Eighth Street. Life re-turned to normal.

But not for long. Unknown to Mary black shadows were gathering over certain people she loved. Terrible heartache was to come to her in the months ahead.

The first dark event was the death of her father in July. Affection was always the most important force with Mary and she had loved him so dearly she had named her firstborn for him. Family ties had been renewed and sweetened by her recent visits to Lexington. Now there was a fundamental break in the old homestead and it would never be the same again. It hurt her deeply.

Mr. Todd's death resulted in the Lincoln family making another journey to Kentucky. By this time Mary had a third sister living in Springfield, her sister Ann, now Mrs. Clark M. Smith. With Mary herself this made four heirs of Mr. Todd in Illinois. When a legal matter arose over their father's will, they selected that excellent lawyer in their own family circle, Mr. A. Lincoln, to go to Lexington to look after their legal interests. Of course he took his family along. So once more the tall gentleman with the short wife and two lively little boys boarded a river steamboat for the long journey.

They had one exciting event on the way. On the Ohio River their boat got into a race with another steamboat. This was thrilling and the passengers lined up at the deck rails to watch and cheer. The Lincoln boat was fired up so vigorously that it ran out of fuel. More firewood must be loaded on from a flatboat as quickly as possible. Mr. Lincoln jumped down, shouted, "Come on boys," and pitched wood with great enthusiasm. But alas, all this noble effort was wasted; the other boat steamed ahead and won the race.

They were all back in Springfield in December. When the new year of 1850 came in, Mary's thoughts were not in harmony with its celebration: her baby Eddie was sick. Loving her children with such passionate intensity, she became almost frantic when they were ill. She always tried her best to keep them well by dosing them with the old-fashioned medicines then considered the right thing. The old account books of a Springfield drugstore show that she bought such items as "Castor Oil," "Calomel," and "Syrup Ipecac." The item "3 sticks Cough Candy" does not sound so bad but one "Bottle Vermifuge" sounds awful! This was horrible-tasting stuff with which all conscientious mothers of that time dosed their children for worms. After one dose the children invariably preferred the worms to the medicine.

Eddie's illness dragged on through January. Hospitals and nurses were not available then as now. Mary cared for her sick child day and night with help from the equally worried father. During this time of strain and anxiety news came of another sad event. Grandmother Parker at Lexington died. She had played an important part in Mary's girlhood. It was to Grandmother Parker she had fled for sympathy when she had rebelled at the strictness of her stepmother. It had been Grandmother Parker who could tell her about her own mother.

Now there were two deaths in the family and Eddie was getting weaker. When would this nightmare end? These were fearful days for the young mother who had been such a lighthearted girl. She and Mr. Lincoln and their doctor did what they could for the sick child but they were helpless. On the bleak winter morning of February 1, Eddie's eyes closed in death.

The world turned black and desolate to Mary. She

did not know how to meet this great tragedy. Worn out with long nursing and torn with grief, she went into one spasm of weeping after another. She was never to learn how to hold back her tears. She could not sleep or eat. Mr. Lincoln, haggard and grieving himself, bent over her pleading, "Eat, Mary, for we must live." In the end it was her love for him and Bobbie, and their need of her, that made her take up normal life once more.

Wise planning took place. The family went to Lexington again that spring, where Mary had a chance to rest and build up after her great sorrow. The wound would always leave a deep scar. Neither she nor Mr. Lincoln could ever forget their regret and longing for the sweet little boy they had lost. Mary would always cry when she talked of him. But she hoped another baby would come to them to take away that empty feeling in her arms.

When they returned to the home on Eighth Street her grief was inevitably renewed. The very house seemed lonely for the sound of Eddie's little voice. The shock of losing her child had increased her nervousness and tension. She knew that summer that she was going to have another baby and while this was what she wanted with her whole heart, her condition added to her strain.

At times that year, perhaps when one of her headaches was coming on, she would go into hysterics, crying out and saying things she did not mean. She had always been excitable but there is no record of her having hysterics before her marriage. She was "beside herself" at these times, which means literally she was not her real self. Mr. Lincoln was aware that it was sickness that caused these outbursts. He would say to the neighbors that Mary was having one of her "nervous spells" or "Mrs. Lincoln is not well today." After the headache or other ailment had passed, she would become calm again and be dreadfully sorry and ashamed for what she had said or done. Mary was not equal physically or emotionally to the strains that were coming to her.

By December the big question in the cottage was which would get there first, Christmas or the new baby. This question was answered on December 21, when another little son was born in the Lincoln home. They named the baby William Wallace after Mary's brother-in-law, Dr. Wallace. Of course they promptly nicknamed him Willie.

Mary, after such a hard year, was slow in regaining her strength after Willie's birth. Mr. Lincoln mentioned in a letter written three weeks later that she was still "sick-abed." But at least on Christmas Day she had another precious child to hold in her arms and this meant everything.

When the new year of 1851 came in, a happy period was beginning for the Lincolns after all their sorrow. Willie was such an adorable baby that he alone would have made home life sweet and interesting. He was a beautiful blue-eyed infant, bright and responsive with coos and smiles. His hair was to be light brown, like his mother's, but as his personality developed through his first year and then his second, Mary began to realize that this child was going to be like his father. Willie had not inherited her high-strung, brittle temperament. He was a well-adjusted little fellow, quick to learn and reason things out for himself, yet very playful and affectionate. Coming as he did after the bitter loss of Eddie and having such an endearing nature, he was almost worshiped by both his father and mother.

The overflowing parental love of Mary and Mr. Lincoln, however, was not completely satisfied. They did so want a little girl too. No one could have had more to say about how wonderful her boys were than Mary, but if she had a little girl she could curl her hair and make her wee dainty frocks. It would be such joy to dress a daughter who would grow up to be interested in clothes and other feminine things that she herself loved. Mr. Lincoln and the boys paid little attention to such things.

Mary had a dear neighbor, Mrs. Sprigg, who had just such a small daughter as she would have liked to have. This little girl's name was Julia and one day Mary invited her to spend the night at the Lincoln home. Julia remembered later the thrill of packing her tiny ruffled nightgown for this adventure of spending the night away from home. She had a good time when she was with Mrs. Lincoln, she said, because "she was the kind of a woman that children liked." Mary petted and played with her and in her anxiety that Julia should not get cold put so many blankets over her that Julia got too hot! Perhaps Mary was "making believe" that night that she had a little daughter.

When Willie's second birthday came around the Lincolns knew they were to have another baby. Surely this time it would be a little girl. Mr. Lincoln had his heart set on it quite as much as Mary. He talked so much about it to some close friends who were traveling with him on the law circuit that they feared he would not be reconciled if this child should prove to be another boy. Surely it was not unreasonable to expect one child out of four to be a girl.

If the baby had arrived four days earlier, that is, on the first of April, it would have been a clear case of the Lincolns' being April-fooled! On April 4 was born, not the expected daughter, but another son. He was to prove such a mischievous little sprite that it seems quite in character that he started out by playing this joke on his parents. They named him Thomas for Mr. Lincoln's humble backwoods father who had died two years before. Mary thus honored her husband's unschooled parent whose pioneer life had been so hard.

The next step was to find a handy nickname. Usually a baby named Thomas becomes Tom or Tommy but not in this case. This latest arrival had a large head on a tiny body, which is the usual pattern of young babies. His father, viewing him one day, probably when Mary was giving him a bath, called him a little tadpole. From that time on he was Tad or Taddie.

There was little or no talk of "bottle babies" at that

time and the formulas of today were unknown. Mary nursed her babies herself. It happened that about the time Tad was born a son was born also to their neighbors, the Dallmans, who lived a few steps away around the corner on Jackson Street. Someone (perhaps it was Mr. Lincoln with a troubled look in his eyes) told Mary that Mrs. Dallman was so ill she was unable to nurse her baby.

All Mary's renewed motherhood rose in response. Her own baby was fed and safe beside her and her neighbor's baby was crying with hunger. They must bring the poor little thing to her; she would nurse both babies. It was Mr. Lincoln who carried the tiny infant from the Dallman home to his wife's bedside. Mary's arms tenderly received him and his pitiful cries were hushed at her breast. She continued to nurse him until Mrs. Dallman was able to do it herself.

Taddie was their last child. The Lincolns were not to have the little daughter they wanted. But they felt very rich in having three boys. Mary said their sons were "the noblest, purest, most talented — that were ever given to parents." This sounds somewhat partial (not to say doubtful), but at least that is the way Mary looked at it.

"We Have Enlarged Our Borders Since You Were Here"

ᴇʀ neighbors did not quite agree with Mary in thinking that her children were so perfect. They said the Lincoln boys were spoiled. This raises the question of how Mary and Mr. Lincoln were bringing up their children and training them in this age when people in general were so strict with their young.

The Lincolns did not believe in whipping. Mr. Lincoln did mention in a letter that Bobbie at the age of three received a spanking for running away from home, but that was all. Mary could not endure the idea of whipping her children. "In the first place," she said, "*they* never required it. A gentle, loving word, was all sufficient with them." Mr. Lincoln expressed the same idea when he said, "Love is the chain whereby to bind a child to its parents."

Willie and Tad grew into two bright, lively, mischievous, affectionate little boys. Willie was a handsome lad and he showed more and more that he had his father's qualities. Tad had dark hair and eyes, a very expressive face, and his mother's quick, excitable disposition. He could not talk as plainly as the other boys because he had a speech defect. When he saw Julia Sprigg's mother, he called her "Mith Spwigg." Other children teased him about his lisp and this made him very angry, for he was easily upset. Most of the time, however, he was a cheerful and lovable little fellow.

The two little brothers were inseparable. Mr. Lincoln would sometimes take them with him to his office when their mother could not be at home with them. He would sit down at his desk and become absorbed in his work while the uninhibited youngsters would pull the books off the shelves, scatter the legal documents, ruin the pens, and spill ink all over the place.

Mr. Lincoln was not at all disturbed by these juvenile activities. He considered them, to repeat his own words, "that sort of mischief that is the offspring of much animal spirits."

If one of the boys did something which was definitely wrong (not merely high-spirited prankishness), the father or mother would talk the matter over with him, letting him state his side of it, and then explain and reason with him until he saw why it was wrong. Both Mary and Mr. Lincoln had the nice trait of understanding how a thing looked to a child. Somehow, in the end, the "gentle, loving words" (and that chain of love) seemed to work about as well as a whip, for the children all developed good consciences.

Mary looked back upon her childhood as desolate because her stepmother had not wanted her. Perhaps this made her even more anxious to be a good mother. She certainly did everything in her power to make her children happy. She read them stories. She taught them dances and merry games and good manners. She gave children's parties for them. There still exists in her flowing handwriting one of the invitations she wrote for Willie's birthday party. Its wording seems old-fashioned and formal now, as most of the writing of that time does today: "Willie Lincoln will be pleased to see you, Wednesday Afternoon at 3 O'clock."

There is no doubt Mary was as devoted a mother as she was a wife. Later she would look back to that time of living in neighborly Springfield with "a nice home — loving husband" and precious children as one of the happiest stages of her life.

When Tad was three Mary made her home even nicer. The roof was raised to make the cottage into the two-story house you see in Springfield today. The enlargement of the house was in keeping with what was happening in general around that time.

Things were getting bigger and better in a number of ways. Travel was a bit easier and quicker now. The magic word "railroad" was on many lips. Tracks were being laid over the land and trains were running, some of them whizzing along at the breath-taking speed of twenty-eight miles an hour! What an improvement that was over travel on a stagecoach! For Mary personally the most important effect of the railroads was that Mr. Lincoln could get home more often at weekends when he was traveling on the law circuit.

All the housewives were rejoicing because gas for lighting was being installed in Springfield. Mary's cousin wrote her daughter about the men digging in the yard to lay gas pipes and said exultingly, "Won't we be light and no lamps to fill either." People were making remarks to each other about what a progressive age they were living in, and Springfield was almost putting on grand airs.

Mr. Lincoln was now both more prominent and more prosperous. He had long since become the senior member of his law firm, with a younger man named Herndon as his junior law partner. It was still necessary to be careful in spending but there was usually a servant in the kitchen now and Mary was properly improving the house to keep up with the improvement in her husband's fortunes. She never forgot that a good wife upholds her husband's interests by doing her part socially.

Mary planned the enlargement of the home as a surprise for Mr. Lincoln, and she probably paid for it herself with a certain amount of money which had come to her from her father. Mr. Lincoln was out of town on the judicial circuit and she asked her good neighbor, Mr. James Gourley, to help her with her pleasant little "conspiracy." He assisted her in making the arrangements with the carpenters and the work was done while Mr. Lincoln was still absent. When he finally returned and came to the corner of Eighth and Jackson Streets, he

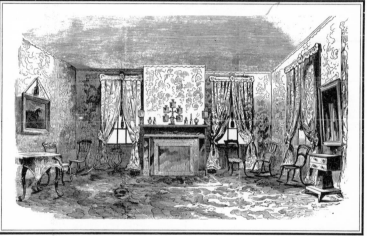

Mary's Arrangement of Her Front Rooms

The parlor, with its ornamental little stove, is above; the family sitting room below. A visitor to the house wrote, "The hand of the domestic artist was everywhere visible. The thought that involuntarily blossomed into speech was — 'What a pleasant home Abe Lincoln has.'"

found his home suddenly grown much taller! He probably stared a moment with an I-can't-believe-my-eyes expression, then, with his usual playfulness, he said to a passerby, "Stranger do you know where Lincoln lives, he used to live here."

Like many men Mr. Lincoln was not especially interested in the fixing up of his home. His mind was on other things, and he took little notice of what he called "flub dubs" around the house. Mary, however, was in her element when, after the home was increased in size, she began to redecorate it. The charge accounts of certain Springfield stores still exist and they show she was selecting and buying new wallpaper at this time. A little later in these faded accounts appear such items as "36 yds. Buff Linen" at twenty-five cents a yard and "36 yds. cotton Damask." Plainly the lady of the house was going to make herself some new curtains. Finally the refurbishing was done and then of course it was time to give a party and let everyone see how fine the house was!

The party was "a very large and I really believe a very handsome entertainment," Mary wrote her sister Emilie a few days afterwards. About five hundred were invited, she continued, "yet owing to an unlucky rain three hundred only favored us by their presence." Many huge parties were being given in Springfield by this time but at least one guest thought that people had more fun at the Lincoln parties than the others. This gentleman remembered how he stood at the dining table heaped up with good things to eat when his host passed by. "Do they give you anything to eat here?" said Mr. Lincoln to him with a genial smile.

One of these big Springfield parties had two small uninvited guests. It happened on the evening when Mr. and Mrs. Dubois, who lived a couple of blocks away on Eighth Street, were having a reception. Mary was dressing for this stately affair with "Delie" Wheelock, a teenage neighbor girl of whom she was fond, to help her. A lady putting on a dress over enormous hoop skirts certainly must have needed help. How could she ever reach over that big bulge to pull her skirt down smoothly in the back?

Delie remembered that the gown Mrs. Lincoln wore that evening was a lovely canary-colored satin with a low neck and short sleeves. It was Delie who later told this story, which may throw some light on the neighbors' conviction that the Lincoln children were spoiled.

About the time Mary was ready, Willie and Tad came home from a taffy pull, smeared with molasses candy from head to foot. Seeing their mother in festive attire they decided they wanted to go to the party too. Their mother said no; they were to stay at home with Robert. At this the two little boys set up a lively howl. Mrs. Lincoln repeated that they could not go, whereupon they began to kick and scream. Just then Mr. Lincoln came in.

"This will never do," he said. "Mary, if you will let the boys go, I will take care of them."

"Why, Father, you know that it is no place for boys to

be. When people give a party like that it is no place for children." Of course by this time the boys had hushed to listen with great interest.

"But," said Father, "I will take them around the back way, and they can stay in the kitchen."

Mary could not hold out against those tears either, so it was decided to take the boys along. Mr. Lincoln talked to them about being good and keeping their promises, while Robert and Delie hurriedly cleaned them up, and dressed them in such haste that Tad's little pants were put on hind side before. He began to cry again about this, because he "couldn't walk good." His father waved a hand at him saying, "Remember, now, remember," and Tad concluded it was not a good time to argue over trifles. Of course the matter ended by Willie and Tad not staying in the kitchen at all but attending the reception itself!

In her letter to "dear Emilie" in which she told about her own big party of three hundred guests, Mary remarked, "You will think we have enlarged our borders since you were here." The loved "Little Sister" had made a visit to Springfield some months before the Lincolns had added to their house. She had grown into a beautiful girl of eighteen by that time and sociable Springfield outdid itself in parties during her stay. With four married sisters living in the town besides numerous cousins, just the family gatherings of relatives sometimes included fifty people.

Mary regarded this half sister, so much younger than

herself, very much as a daughter and so did Mr. Lincoln. Emilie spent a great deal of time in the Lincoln home during her six-month visit, sharing the family's daily living, and fortunately she recorded what she saw and heard.

Emilie had described how pretty her sister looked when she came to Lexington seven years before. Now, watching Mary going about her home, Emilie found her "gay and light-hearted, hopeful and happy." She observed that Mary would keep looking out of the window when it was time for her husband to come home. Emilie's keen eyes also noticed that the absent-minded Mr. Lincoln required almost as much looking after as the children in the matter of dress, that Mary often had to run after him with his umbrella when he started out on a rainy day, or with his muffler when it was cold.

Emilie heard the stories, jokes, and household expressions that exist in any family. She was told with much laughing about the time when Mr. Lincoln spilled the baby. This happened when the boys were very young. Mr. Lincoln, acting as baby-sitter while his wife went to church one Sunday morning, put them in their little wagon and slowly pulled them up and down the street in front of the house. He drew the wagon with one hand while he held a book with the other, so that he could read at the same time he amused the children.

Now Mr. Lincoln, when he was absorbed in a book, was completely unaware of what was going on around him. One of the babies fell out and lay squalling on the sidewalk while his father paced on with his nose in the book. Just at that moment Mary came walking down the street from church.

Of course she was panicky at seeing her baby sprawled out on the ground and crying. She went into hysterics, screaming loudly and scolding Mr. Lincoln as she ran to help her child. There was not much Mr. Lincoln could say in his own defense, so he hastily departed. Afterwards they could laugh about the incident, in which the joke really was on both of them — on him for being so absent-minded and on her for giving way to her fright and anger in front of the neighbors.

Mr. Lincoln's absent-mindedness frequently gave trouble in the household. He could never be counted on to come home to meals on time. Mary would sometimes scold him for this shortcoming by imitating Mammy Sally and threatening that Mr. Jay Bird would fly to the bad place and tell Mr. Satan about "you-all's sins." "Ole man Satan's done got the latch pulled," Mary would say, shaking her finger at her husband, "caze he keeps track of the time an' when Mr. Jay pecks three times, the do' flies open."

Emilie heard one of these gay exchanges of mimicry. She was in the Lincoln home and the family were assembled for supper, all except Mr. Lincoln. He did not come. Half an hour went by, then an hour, then an hour and a half. Emilie and Bob frankly said they were hungry but Mrs. Lincoln felt that they ought to wait for her husband.

It was two hours before he leisurely strolled in, completely unaware that he was late. Mary said to him as they went to the table, "I am afraid the chickens are burned to a crisp." This time Mr. Lincoln was the first one to use the Mammy Sally imitation. With his eyes twinkling, he pointed his finger at Mary and said, "Nem mine! Mr. Jay's gwine tell ole man Satan that Mary sets her hungry husband down to burned up vittals just caze he's two minutes late." "Two minutes!" cried Mary and Emilie together, "two hours you mean." "Nem mine," said Mr. Lincoln in high good humor, "just bring on the cinders and see how quickly they will disappear."

One day Emilie witnessed another delightful scene between the Lincolns. Mary did a great deal of sewing, making her own clothes and even Mr. Lincoln's shirts. She had just completed a new dress, a lovely white silk with blue brocaded flowers scattered over it, and like any woman with a new frock, she was eager to wear it. Luckily they were all invited over to sister Lizzie Edwards's house for supper that evening, so on went the white silk gown over the spreading hoop skirts.

When Mr. Lincoln came home from his office she reminded him to change his clothes for the party. He evidently noticed the flush of pride on his wife's face and also how pretty she looked in the new gown, for he smiled and said, "Fine feathers enough on you to make fine birds of both of us." Noticing the white silk more closely, he added, "Those posies on your dress are the color of your eyes." Mary dimpled with pleasure and remarked to Emilie, "You see, Emilie, I am training my husband to see color. I do not think he knew pink from blue when I married him."

First and last there was much talk of pretty clothes while Emilie was with the Lincolns. One Sunday morning she went to church with Mary and the eyes of both sisters took in the splendors of the bonnet worn by the governor's beautiful daughter, Lydia Matteson. Coming home from church Mary said, "Emilie, you are just as pretty as Lydia, but I do not like your bonnet." That week the older sister took great pleasure in selecting a white velvet bonnet with lovely white plumes on it as a gift to Emilie. When next Sunday morning came around and the family went to church, there was no doubt that Emilie far outshone the governor's daughter!

That was a happy winter which Emilie spent in Springfield. She was still there when spring again brought its many colors to the prairie. The Lincolns could now afford a carriage, and the young girl always remembered the drives out into the level countryside to gather great armfuls of its gorgeous wildflowers. Bob, now going on twelve, went with them and would gallantly help the hoop-skirted ladies in and out of the carriage, according to the good manners his mother had taught him.

Emilie went back to Lexington later that spring. It had been her good fortune to look into the Lincoln home at one of its happiest periods. The 1850's were rich years for Mary and Abraham. All the while, unknown to them in their quiet, small-town existence, the double line of their destiny was winding its way toward that sudden turn upward which would take them to the dizzy heights of the Presidency.

· 12 ·

Excitement in the House on Eighth Street

*E*ARLY one morning before the Lincolns were astir, there came a violent knocking at the door. The pounding indicated that the matter was urgent. What could be wrong? Were any of the relatives in trouble or was someone near to death and wanting lawyer Lincoln to make a will?

Mr. Lincoln, probably in a dressing gown, went to the door as quickly as he could. A messenger stood on the doorstep. He explained that he had been sent by the sheriff. Three men, all very drunk, had, so to speak, been painting the town red the night before. They had smashed in the entire front of a grocery store and committed other acts of vandalism until the sheriff had arrested them just before daybreak. He was holding them now in his office, and he had sent the messenger to Mr. Lincoln because one of the men was his junior law partner, William Herndon. Unless Mr. Lincoln could raise one hundred dollars right away, his law partner would be thrown into jail.

This was all distressing news to Mr. Lincoln. He hated the fact that his law partner went on these drunken sprees, and where could he get one hundred dollars on such short notice? He hastily dressed and then went to the home of a well-to-do man for whom he had done a service. In great embarrassment he explained his before-breakfast visit and asked for the required amount. The gentleman was able to give it to him and Mr. Lincoln quickly took it to the sheriff's office. The money paid for the damage done and Mr. Herndon was saved from going to jail.

The incident introduces a person who, unknown to her, was to affect Mary's life in a terrible way. All she knew then was that she did not consider Herndon fit to be her husband's partner. Mr. Lincoln deserved a more reliable partner than one who got drunk and made a public spectacle of himself. Mary probably had some emphatic things to say about this occurrence when Mr. Lincoln came home that day. Suppose this had happened when he was out of town and Herndon was in charge of the Lincoln and Herndon law office. He could not be trusted not to get drunk and Mary detested drunkenness.

She found many of Herndon's other traits distasteful also. He was a roughhewn, coarse-talking, eccentric man who was not acceptable in her social circle or to her. He had a way of taking up any new or flighty notion that came along and talking about it endlessly until another new idea appeared to engage his attention. What must have angered her particularly was his attitude toward religion. Mary was sincerely religious and found great comfort in going to church on Sundays and sitting in the family pew, which can still be seen in Springfield. Herndon scoffed at churchgoing and Christianity. He was not a man for whom she could have respect.

Mr. Lincoln knew Herndon's weaknesses thoroughly and he did not like them either. But Herndon had his desirable traits too: he was smart, worked hard, and was good at doing the routine tasks which fell to a junior partner in a law office. The fatherly Mr. Lincoln had become interested in Herndon when he was a struggling young man and he realized that Herndon needed someone to guide and steady him. He once said to Herndon that he would go far "unless you allow your mind to be improperly directed." Herndon's increasing peculiarities at times caused the senior partner other embarrassing situations. Knowing how gossipy and full of notions he was, Mr. Lincoln was careful never to tell him anything about his personal affairs.

Some of these views may have been well argued between Mary and her husband on the day that began with that urgent knocking at the door. The loss of the hundred dollars undoubtedly worried her. Mr. Lincoln often spoke of how poor they were and she had worked hard and gone without things she wanted in order to economize. She could think of better ways to spend a hundred dollars than to keep that "crazy drinking law partner" (as she once called Herndon) out of jail.

However, she did not see the junior partner often. He rarely had occasion to come to the Lincoln home and she seldom went to the office. She treated him politely when they met but he figured very little in her thoughts at this time. Nobody dreamed that in the future he would be cast in the role of villain in Mary's life drama and would inflict upon her one of the strangest and most cruel wrongs in history.

In the expanding 1850's there were many kinds of excitement in the house on Eighth Street. The same fall in which Emilie had come to visit Springfield had seen the exciting activities of Mr. Lincoln's running for office again. He wanted terribly to be chosen United States Senator and campaigned to this end in what he afterwards called an "agony" of endeavor. Mary, believing in his great qualities, longed for his election with all her heart. Hopes and fears were at fever heat in the Lincoln home.

It was a hard blow to both of them when he was defeated. He had come very close to winning the election and that seemed to make the defeat even harder. Mr. Lincoln was greatly let down and so was Mary. She was a good soldier, however, and held her chin up and did not talk of her disappointment to others. She still believed, in spite of this setback, that her husband would one day rise to the Presidency. Helped perhaps by her optimism, he soon overcame his "blues" and continued to take an active part in politics, making many speeches.

After this jolt things settled back again into the pleasant pattern of small-town living. Mary awoke each morning to the various tasks that make up any housewife's day, letting the dog out, watching the children for sneezes and sniffles, getting them fed and the two older ones off to school, checking that her husband took his umbrella with him to the office if it was rainy, planning three meals a day. She usually had a servant now, often an untrained one from a foreign country. One of these, a Portuguese girl, left delightful descriptions of the mistress and master of the house. Mrs. Lincoln, she said in her appealing accent, "taka no sassy talk, but if you good to her, she good to you. You gotta good friend." About Mr. Lincoln she added, "He so kind. . . . When he passa me, he patta my shoulder. . . . Mr. Lincoln no verra style. He just common, like some one that is poor."

Mary's neighbors figured largely in the pattern of her days. The good people of Springfield helped each other. Mary looked after the neighbor children when they played in the Lincoln back yard and the neighbors in turn looked after hers when the playing was in their back yards. It was as a good neighbor that she had nursed the Dallman baby at her breast. That baby grew into a little boy and then died, just as Eddie Lincoln had died. When the Dallmans returned to their house after the funeral, Mary, her eyes filled with tears, prepared a tray of food, making it as appetizing as she could with her best dishes, and Mr. Lincoln carried it over to the grieved parents. He and Mary knew only too well what that return to the empty home meant.

Likewise they shared happy events with their neighbors, rejoicing over the birth of a fine son or daughter and going to parties, dinners, "strawberry festivals," and weddings.

Thus life in the home on Eighth Street hummed on like a kind of music with various sharps and flats. Mary continued to have her headaches and other illnesses, especially at times of overwork or strain, and occasionally her nerves would spill over in fussing, as with many overburdened housewives. Once in a while she would become hysterical and give way to an outburst of scolding words. Mr. Lincoln knew this happened because she was not well and, as he said to a neighbor, "It does her lots of good and it doesn't hurt me a bit." Such moments of discord were like static against the music of their devoted family life; back of the temporary disturbance the music flowed on, strong, sure, and unchanged.

By 1857 exciting events for the Lincolns began to take on larger dimensions. In the summer of that year Mr. Lincoln had to go east on important legal business and he took his travel-loving wife along. In September, Mary wrote Emilie an enthusiastic account of this trip. By this time the loved "Little Sister" had married a young Kentucky lawyer named Ben Hardin Helm. He had visited the Lincolns in Springfield and they had taken him to their hearts, rejoicing that Emilie had found such a fine and lovable husband.

I *Mary*

"We visited Niagara, Canada, New York & other points of interest," wrote Mary to Emilie. The sight of "the large steamers at the New York landing, ready for their European voyage," she said, awakened a great yearning to cross that wide ocean and visit foreign shores. But Mr. Lincoln was still too poor to afford that. Out of her happy wifehood she would make teasing remarks to him. "I often laugh," she wrote, "& tell Mr. L — that I am determined my next husband *shall be rich*."

(One day Mary would get her wish to go abroad on a great steamer. But when that day came it would not be so much going for the love of travel as a fleeing from her own country.)

The summer following the journey east Mr. Lincoln again ran for United States Senator. He was running against Stephen A. Douglas, Mary's old beau, and never was there a more exciting campaign. The two men, both wonderful speakers, met in seven Illinois towns to debate with each other. Politics, always hot, had now reached the boiling point because people were stirred up over the question of slavery. The nation was dividing into the South, which had slaves, and the North, which was against slavery. In June that year Mr. Lincoln made a speech in which he said, " 'A house divided against itself cannot stand.' I believe this government cannot endure, permanently half *slave* and half *free*." This was to become a life-and-death question to the United States. Our great Civil War was to be fought to keep our nation from this dividing which would lead to its fall.

People flocked from miles around to hear Mr. Lincoln and Mr. Douglas debate. Each town held carnival while they were there with what Mr. Lincoln called "fizzle-gigs and fire-works." There were barbecues, ice cream festivals, the ringing of courthouse bells, parades to the music of brass bands, and most striking of all, torchlight processions in which a long line of dark figures moved by, each holding up a torch of flame against the blackness of the night.

It was Mary's lot to have to stay at home with the children until the last debate. She was passionately interested in every detail of what was happening and went around expressing her confidence in Mr. Lincoln on all sides. When someone mentioned Mr. Douglas one day she said, "Mr. Lincoln may not be as handsome a figure, but the people are perhaps not aware that his heart is as large as his arms are long." Her pride in him was like a flying banner. "Mr. Douglas is a very little, *little* giant by the side of my tall Kentuckian," she exclaimed, "and intellectually my husband towers above Douglas just as he does physically."

While out on his travels during the eight weeks of these debates Mr. Lincoln mentioned to a friend his wife's boosting confidence in him. He was often weighed down with the same kind of self-doubting which he had felt during his courting of Mary and he told this friend he was not sure he was qualified for the United States

Senate. "Mary insists, however," he continued, "that I am going to be Senator and President of the United States, too." He laughed aloud at the very idea.

Mary got a taste of the "fizzle-gigs and fire-works" when her husband came home for the weekend on September 25. That evening a great crowd of people assembled in front of their home and serenaded Mr. Lincoln with a brass band. He made a little speech to them and the house almost shook with their deafening cheers. Willie and Tad, wide-eyed with enthusiasm, joined in, of course, and yelled with all their might. The pleasure of this acclaim for her husband thrilled Mary beyond words. She did not know that before long she, the children, and the very timbers of the house itself would have to get used to this sort of excitement.

Mary did have the thrill of attending the last debate which was at Alton, Illinois. It must have given her a strange feeling to see those two contrasting figures on the platform, her tall, lean husband and the short, compact Mr. Douglas matching their powerful wits against each other. Eighteen years before they had both been her beaux when she was the gay little Miss Todd. Life was more serious now when these two were debating grave questions concerned with the nation's safety. She heard Mr. Lincoln again compare that nation with a house which cannot stand if it be divided against itself.

The campaign ended with a giant rally and torchlight parade in Springfield on October 30. Three days later, on an Election Day as dark and gloomy as the result it brought, Mr. Lincoln was defeated.

It was a horrible disappointment. But that line of the Lincoln destiny had not lost its way. People all over the land had read Mr. Lincoln's speeches and had become aware that a country lawyer in Illinois could think clearly and deeply on the problems facing the nation. Mary's husband had lost this chance to become Senator but he had gained in the chance to become President.

Mary enjoyed writing letters and wrote many of them. You can follow what was happening in these letters. They give glimpses of her in various situations. One written in 1859 shows her as an intensely anxious mother sending a distress signal to her husband, who was out of town and hard to reach.

The letter was to a Springfield friend who was going to Chicago that day. Mary wrote that if he "should meet Mr. L — there, will you say to him, that our *dear little Taddie*, is quite sick." She added that the doctor feared "*lung* fever" (pneumonia) and "it would be a comfort" to have Mr. Lincoln come home as soon as he could. Tad recovered, but these dark crises of the children's illnesses were an agony to both parents after their loss of Eddie. Within the following year Willie had a severe case of scarlet fever.

Another letter of Mary's written in the summer of 1859 is in much happier mood. It shows her going off on a long trip surrounded by friends and loving every minute of it. We "travelled *eleven hundred* miles, with a party of eighteen," she said. "*Words* cannot express what a merry time, we had, the gayest pleasure party, I have ever seen." She explained to this same friend that she now had a reliable maid with whom she could leave the younger children and Robert had gone East to college that year, adding, "I miss Bob, so much, that I do not feel settled down, as much as I used to & find myself going on trips quite frequently."

She was not to feel "settled down" in Springfield again. Too many things were happening now. The following February, Mr. Lincoln gave a speech at the Cooper Union in New York which rapidly became famous and which made many more people aware that this man from Illinois talked like a statesman. After that, events moved swiftly to a date now set down in history, May 18, 1860.

On that day a great political convention was being held in Chicago, and the town of Springfield was holding its breath waiting for the news. Mr. Lincoln was out with friends, all of them keyed up with expectancy, and Mary was at home, her mind on fire with exciting hopes. About noon the booming of a hundred guns began to shake the little town. Did Mary's heart almost stand still at the sound, knowing its great significance? The convention had nominated Mr. Lincoln as the Republican candidate for President of the United States.

Mr. Lincoln's rejoicing friends gathered around him to congratulate him. But dear as these neighbors were, they were not the ones with whom he wanted first to share this news. He said to them as he started toward home, "There's a little woman down at our house would like to hear this. I'll go down and tell her." You can imagine the happy scene that took place inside the front door which bore the nameplate *A. Lincoln.*

From that time on the house on Eighth Street knew nothing but excitement. It grew accustomed to having great crowds in front of it, with band music, speeches and resounding hurrahs for "Old Abe." In August as many as six thousand people marched past in one of these great parades, with music, cheers, banners and posters borne aloft, and one fascinating float after another. Rally by rally the campaign moved on toward Election Day, November 6. Mr. Lincoln, hard-driven by the demands upon him, was discouraged at times but Mary's confidence rode high; she was sure he would win the election.

On the evening of Election Day he stayed down town in the telegraph office with a group of his friends to listen to the election returns as they came over the wires. Outside in the public square a huge crowd was gathered. To the group in the telegraph office the returns came slowly. Time went on and still it was not possible to know who would win. One of Mr. Lincoln's friends finally remarked that "if we get New York that settles it." The hour grew late.

Suddenly the man receiving the telegrams sat up as if electrified. A message was coming through saying that

Mr. Lincoln had carried New York. In wild, confused rejoicing the men rushed in single file down the narrow stairs to tell the crowd outside. In front of the public square ten thousand people went wild. They were shouting, singing, throwing up their hats and slapping each other on the back. But Mr. Lincoln was not among them; he was hurrying toward home. He had said to a friend as he left the scene, "I guess I'll go down and tell Mary about it."

These are the words with which he told her: "Mary, Mary! *we are elected!*"

ERHAPS for an instant husband and wife clung to each other wordlessly, too deeply moved to speak. Then, after her long wait, excited activity came to Mary. Mr. Lincoln took her down town to see the rejoicing. The scene around the public square was described as "perfectly *wild*." The great crowd was "*singing, yelling! shouting!! The boys (not children) dancing. Old men, young, middle aged, clergymen and all!*" Nobody was thinking of sleep that dazzling night. Mary's face was radiant with pride and joy.

In the days that followed it seemed as if neither she nor her husband could get a moment to themselves. Friends and neighbors crowded in at all hours to offer congratulations. One of them after such a visit wrote a letter telling how the Lincolns were taking their sudden glory. "Mr. L. has not altered one bit," she said, "he amused us nearly all the evening telling funny stories and cracking jokes. I could hardly realize that I was sitting in the august presence of a *real live* President.

Mrs. L. is just as agreeable as ever, does not put on any airs at all but is as pleasant and talkative and entertaining as she can be." Another letter mentioned how she was telling friends that they must come to visit in the White House.

The days were going by in a blur of excitement. Now that Mr. Lincoln was President-elect, it was as if great searchlights had been turned on him and his family. Artists flocked to town to sketch and paint his portrait, newspapermen came to interview him, office-seekers came to ask political appointments. His mail became enormous, letters of all kinds arrived and various presents, among them "a very elegant hat." Mr. Lincoln, with his usual love of fun, tried it on before a mirror with great ceremony while Mary looked on with smiling interest. After studying his reflection in the mirror with mock seriousness, he turned to her and said with a twinkle, "Well, wife, there is one thing likely to come out of this scrape, any how. We are going to have some *new clothes!*"

He did not need to tell Mary she was going to get some new clothes. That was one thing she was sure to think of herself. It had not been easy for her to do without handsome clothes in those early, scrimping years of her marriage. Now in her triumphant elation, she felt she could at last have everything she wanted. Was not her husband going to be President? She must, of course, do her part by wearing clothes appropriate for the First Lady of the land.

Springfield's small-town shops were not to be considered. She went to New York early in January 1861 to buy what might be called her White House trousseau. Salesmen showed her costly materials, furs, and jewelry beyond her wildest dreams, and brushed aside the high prices by opening charge accounts for the wife of the President-elect. A charge account has a magic way of making payment seem a far-off, unreal thing that need not be bothered with at the moment. Mary had good taste and bought lovely things but she purchased far more than was necessary and ran up huge bills. It was the first noteworthy example of her weakness for extravagant buying, which was to increase.

Robert, who was attending Harvard, was to meet her and return with her to Springfield. Meanwhile Mr. Lincoln was finding the home on Eighth Street a very dull and lonesome place while "Mother" was away. Not knowing exactly what day she would return, he went to the railroad station three snowy nights in succession hoping his wife and son would come on the evening train. You can picture the tall figure in the dimness watching the passengers get off, hoping to see among them a bright-faced little woman accompanied by an almost grown-up son. Finally, on January 25, they arrived, and then Mr. Lincoln found his home was suddenly full of life and color again as Mary told of the wonderful time she had had in New York.

But now that home must be broken up. The house was to be rented and already the furniture was adver-

TADDIE   WILLIE   BOB

Mary's Boys

Willie was exactly like his father, Tad was a mixture of both parents, and Bob "took after" his mother's side of the house.

tised for sale: "Parlor and Chamber Sets, Carpets, Sofas, Chairs, Wardrobes, Bureaus, Bedsteads, Stoves." There was not a piece of this furniture which could not have told its own little story of the family living in that house.

For Mary now, in spite of her thrills, there were moments of sadness at this giving up of her home and leaving her loved friends and neighbors. At times she felt a sudden chilling fear. The South did not like it that this Mr. Lincoln, a man from the West who was opposed to slavery, had been elected President. South Carolina had withdrawn from the United States in December and word kept coming during January that one or another of the Southern states had also seceded. The dividing of the Union which Mr. Lincoln had said would lead to its downfall was taking place. It was a time of fearful crisis, war was threatened between the North and South of the country.

Early in January, Mary received from South Carolina what was probably intended to be a ghastly Christmas present. It was a painting showing Lincoln with a rope around his neck, his feet chained and his body covered with tar and feathers, an object to give a nervous and devoted wife horrible nightmares.

She had a worrying decision to make about the journey to Washington. She and Mr. Lincoln were not in agreement about it. He was going a long, roundabout way so that he could make appearances at many different places, and the question was whether she should leave with him or meet him with the two younger children in

New York. Rumors were afloat about intended attacks on the President-elect on his trip east. Mary's friends told her of these rumors as an argument for her not going with him. This had the opposite effect from what was intended. Mary answered with considerable spirit that she "would see Mr. Lincoln on to Washington, danger or no danger." Her husband, on the other hand, did not want her to take any unnecessary risks.

Finally a dispatch came from General Winfield Scott in Washington saying it would be safer for Lincoln on the trip "to be surrounded by his family." That settled the matter for Mary; after that message nothing could keep her from going with him.

It seems evident that she made her plans without telling him what she intended to do, knowing he would oppose them for her own safety. She went to the railway depot that rainy morning of February 11, when Mr. Lincoln said good-by to Springfield, and saw him off, Robert going with him. A great crowd of his old friends and neighbors were at the station, and as Mr. Lincoln stood on the train platform and looked out over the loved, familiar faces, his own face was filled with deep emotion. It was not only that he had to say farewell to these dear people; a way of life which he had found good was over.

He began to speak to these friends out of the deep feelings in his heart. To them and to their kindness he owed everything, he said. He had lived among them for nearly a quarter of a century. This was the place where his children had been born and where one was buried. He was now leaving, he told them, to face a task "greater than that which rested upon Washington." He knew he must try to keep his country from that dividing which would lead to its fall. It was only with God's help, he said, that he could accomplish that task. "Trusting in Him, who can go with me, and remain with you and be everywhere for good, let us confidently hope that all will yet be well. To His care commending you, as I hope in your prayers you will commend me, I bid you an affectionate farewell."

The train, with bright flags and streamers waving from engine and cars, moved down the track. Standing in the crowd, Mary was among those who wiped away tears. She comforted herself with the plan she had made. With Willie and Tad in tow, she was going to take a train that evening which would catch up with her husband's train before it left Indianapolis the next day.

She was very nervous and tense on that overtaking journey for fear she would not reach Indianapolis in time. This is a further indication that Mr. Lincoln did not know of her plan. If he had known she was coming she would have been sure that he would wait for her.

As it was, she and the children did barely reach his train and board it before it pulled out. You can imagine the scene when, with sparkling eyes, the three entered the car where "Father" sat all unsuspecting. The expression on his face must have been a study with mingled

surprise, delight, and a certain amused acknowledgment
that "Mother" had "put one over" on him.

Perhaps the first cry of the invading three was
"Happy birthday!" It was February 12 and Mr. Lincoln
was fifty-two years old on that day. He was much
tickled about what he called his wife's "popping up"
like this and the incident became a merry topic for them
to tease each other about as the train moved on.

Mary found the inside of the train as festive as its flag-
waving exterior. The Presidential car was furnished with
a luxury that could not have failed to delight her. The
side walls beneath the windows were covered with crimson plush and between the windows hung heavy blue
silk studded with silver stars. At each end of the car appeared the stars and stripes of the national flag, two large
crossed banners of rich silk, while patriotic red, white,
and blue festoons hung from the ceiling.

Surrounded by her family and the group of special
friends aboard the train, Mary's spirit rose as on that
other journey which she had called "the gayest pleasure
party" which she had ever seen. It was all that, and in
addition the husband in whom she had always had so
much faith and pride had now become the most important man in the country. The train would stop at the
various stations where great crowds would be assembled
to see him. Mr. Lincoln had to appear on the back platform to bow and say a few words. At Ashtabula, Ohio,
the cheering people called for Mrs. Lincoln too and her
husband, his face crinkling in a smile, told them he

"didn't believe he could induce her to come out. In fact he could say that he never succeeded very well in getting her to do anything she didn't want to do." The crowd laughed delightedly.

At another station he did bring Mary out on the platform with him. They stood there, the tall man and the little woman who hardly came to his shoulder, while he told the people he had concluded to give them "the long and the short of it!" Again the crowd roared its enjoyment.

Since Mr. Lincoln gave little thought to his clothes, it had always been his wife's responsibility to see that he was dressed properly. Somehow in the rush of events before leaving Springfield he had come away wearing an old hat and worn overcoat. Mary did something about it with the result that shortly after the train left Utica, New York, a servant entered the car with a handsome new broadcloth overcoat over his arm and a new hatbox in his hand. After that, as a newspaper said, "Mr. Lincoln has looked fifty per cent. better."

Those happy-go-lucky pranksters Willie and Tad were having the time of their lives on the journey. People, as they usually do, had selected a handy nickname for their President and Mr. Lincoln was often referred to as "Old Abe." The boys delighted in asking strangers, "Do you want to see Old Abe?" and then pointing out someone else.

The crowds at the stations were greatly interested in the Presidential family aboard. At Poughkeepsie, seeing

Mary through the train window, the people started cheering her. She promptly raised the window and smilingly returned the greeting. "Where are the children? Show us the children?" shouted someone outside. Mary called seventeen-year-old Robert to the window and he also was cheered. "Have you any more on board?" was the next shout. "Yes, here's another," called Mary gaily, turning to get Tad. Tad promptly threw himself on the floor and stuck to it like a doormat, so that Mary had to get the idea across that their youngest refused to be exhibited.

How did Mary and her husband appear to the eyes of the curious people gazing at them? A man in New York remarked that Mr. Lincoln was "*not* so *bad* looking as they say," and that Mrs. Lincoln was "a plump, amiable, modest, pleasant, round faced, agreeable woman, with no silly airs." Both were taking their public appearances in their stride and were making an excellent impression.

So the train tour went on strenuously but merrily until they reached Pennsylvania. There Mary received a shock that gave her a dark foretaste of things to come.

She was quietly taken aside and informed that Allan Pinkerton, a Chicago detective, believed there was a plot to assassinate Lincoln when he went through Baltimore. Those in charge of his safety had decided he must be taken secretly through that city by night, ahead of his scheduled trip. Mr. Lincoln, knowing how upset and distressed she would be at his leaving her, insisted that she be told, even though the matter required the utmost secrecy.

Mary, emotionally unstable as she was, almost went into hysterics. Here was the threat of violent death to the husband who was dearer to her than life itself. She had hurried her plans in order to be at his side in possible danger; now she must remain behind and keep up appearances while he was smuggled through the hostile city. Because it was for his safety, she faced it, asking only that his most trustworthy and devoted guard go with him.

One can imagine the strain of that long night for her lying sleepless in an agony of fear. Mr. Lincoln had to change stations in Baltimore and she could picture him being driven in a carriage through the dark streets where might lurk those men who wanted to kill him.

Morning brought the relieving word that he had arrived safely in Washington. Then Mary had the courage to go with her children and the rest of the party through Baltimore by day according to the original schedule. The evening of February 23 found the Lincolns united at Willard's Hotel in Washington, where they were to stay until the Inauguration. But Mary, who had grown up with a feeling of insecurity, now had to live with an underlying fear for her husband's life. That terrible dread was the background for the days and months ahead of her.

Inauguration Day, March 4, dawned cloudy. Soon, however, the anxious eyes of the waiting crowds saw the weather clear, and the sun shone down as they watched the colorful Inaugural parade moving along Pennsylvania Avenue toward the Capitol. A great platform had been erected on its east front for the Inaugural ceremony. Behind it rose, not the low rounded top of the Capitol which Mary had so often seen from the windows of their boardinghouse when they had been in Washington more than thirteen years before, but a new tall dome only half complete. Its top part was missing just as those Southern states which had withdrawn were missing from the Union. That half-built dome was like a symbol of the United States, which was dividing and threatening never again to be a complete whole.

Mary sat on the platform back of the group of dignitaries around her husband at the front. She could see the back of his head with the dear, familiar shagginess of the dark hair. The young Mary Todd whose love of the dramatic had once been thrilled at being in a little play at Madame Mentelle's was now an important figure on a real-life stage which held the eyes of the nation. Soon she was to be at the center of the tremendous drama in that nation's history when it was engaged in the life-and-death struggle of its great Civil War. Fate henceforth was seemingly to delight in placing her in circumstances which were the very essence of drama.

Mr. Lincoln still hoped that the war could be averted. As he spoke to the great assembled crowd Mary could hear his earnest voice pleading with the inflamed South: "We are not enemies, but friends. We must not be en-

Unfinished Dome

The incomplete dome of the Capitol, which rose behind Lincoln at his first Inauguration, was like a symbol of the broken Union, a nation still to be welded.

emies. Though passion may have strained, it must not break our bonds of affection." His words were like the stretching out of appealing hands to the South in which both he and Mary had been born.

Thus Mary on that memorable fourth of March, 1861, saw her cherished prediction of the years come true: Mr. Lincoln was now President. The day ended with the great Inaugural Ball. It was late in the evening when the Presidential party reached the festive hall, elaborately decorated with shields and flags and brilliantly illuminated for the occasion. The band struck up "Hail Columbia" as the party promenaded from one end of the hall to the other. The new President with two dignitaries led the procession, and behind him, her heart beating high in response to the music and the splendor, came the new First Lady. Circumstances, as usual, had selected her partner in that parade with an eye to the dramatic. Beside her, her hand resting on his arm, walked her old beau, Stephen A. Douglas, the "Little Giant."

A striking couple they were for the crowd to look upon. Mary was dressed with a richness she could hardly have dreamed of in her early married days. Her great bell-shaped hoop skirt was so huge its diameter at the bottom must have been almost as wide as she was tall. Her dress had probably taken in its making all of the thirty square yards of silk which the extreme fashions of the time recommended. It had a low neck and short sleeves which showed her white shoulders and arms to great advantage, and there were roses against the tiny close-fitting bodice and roses in the rich brown hair above the glowing face.

Mary danced the quadrille with Mr. Douglas later in the evening. Certainly there were many things these two could have talked about as they touched hands in the dance. Did he perhaps, glancing at the roses in her hair, speak of that long-ago day when they had walked laughing along a Springfield street, his powerful head adorned with her wreath of flowers?

In the intense excitement of Inauguration Day there may have been no time for Mary to look back to the long way she had come. That night for the first time she and her husband slept beneath the roof of the great white mansion at 1600 Pennsylvania Avenue. More than thirteen years before, Congressman Lincoln and his wife had gazed upon that historic White House with awe and a vague, improbable longing. And now it was to be their home for the next four years.

14

Shadowed Pomp and Circumstance

THE Inauguration was on a Monday. In spite of her late hours the night before, Mary rose early on Tuesday morning and finished breakfast shortly after eight o'clock. She was standing at a window upstairs, looking out on her new surroundings, when a knock came at the door. The visitor was a mulatto woman named Elizabeth Keckley who had come to apply for the position of dressmaker to the new First Lady.

With Mary were her sister Mrs. Edwards and several other women relatives who had come to Washington to attend the Inauguration and were now guests in the White House. Later Mrs. Keckley described the intimate group she saw before her, and in so doing she answered the question, What did ladies at that time wear when they were not dressed in hoop skirts? Certainly nobody could do much around the house trailing the responsibility of all those yards of dress goods draped over crinoline and hoops. "Mrs. Lincoln this morning," said

Elizabeth Keckley, "was dressed in a cashmere wrapper, quilted down the front; and she wore a simple headdress. The other ladies wore morning robes."

Mary greeted Mrs. Keckley "warmly" and engaged her to make "a bright rose-colored moire-antique" dress for a reception which was to take place the next Friday. That bit of business settled, Mary, like any woman who has moved to a new home and taken a new position, wished to investigate the house in which she was to live and to find out what her duties were.

She and the visiting relatives later that morning went over the White House from top to bottom. They found furnishings amazingly worn and shabby. Cleaning, repairing, and much new furniture were badly needed. Many women would have quailed at the responsibility of refurbishing the White House, but Mary was ready for it with her usual enthusiasm. She loved to shop for beautiful household things almost as much as she did for lovely clothes.

There was more, however, to her feeling about it than mere pleasure. It was her duty as the President's wife to select the new furnishings. The bill would be paid with money appropriated by Congress. Mary wanted with all her heart to carry out her duties in the best way possible and to fill her new position fittingly and graciously.

The little group of women entered the enormous East Room which was the state parlor of the White House. It was here that the big official receptions would take place when the President and First Lady would stand under the stately chandeliers to greet hundreds of people. The carpet was worn by the thousands of feet which had walked over it. It would be her task to select the new one.

They also inspected the three smaller parlors on the south side of the White House, the Green Room (which, for a tragic reason, Mary would not enter again after the first year), the lovely oval Blue Room, and the Red Room. The last was to become Mary's favorite place for receiving small groups after she had had the furniture done over in crimson satin and gold damask and bought a rich red carpet for the floor. There was a grand piano in this room and a full-length portrait of George Washington.

Continuing their survey of the ground floor, the women went through the state and family dining rooms on the west side. Beyond this was the conservatory, where Mary could step into the moist, green, and fragrant world of growing plants. Loving flowers as she loved all beautiful things, she could have as many as she wished now for the White House parties and she was to delight in presenting bouquets to her friends. The bedrooms on the second floor were on the west side, while the President's and other offices were at the other end over the East Room.

Before the first day was over Mary had learned what having Mr. Lincoln's office under the same roof as his home would mean. By afternoon the place was filled with all kinds of people wanting to see the new President. The halls and even the stairway were crowded with them, so that members of the family often had to push their way through them as they went from one part of the house to another. Mary was never to get away from the pressure of those crowds in the White House.

Custom required the President and his wife to give a certain number of entertainments. The reception on Friday, March 8, was the first of a regular series of Friday evening receptions open to the public. When the hour came for the First Lady to dress for this occasion, Mrs. Keckley had not yet arrived with the moire costume. Mary, already tense with the prospect of facing hundreds of strange people, was upset and nervous over this delay. Mrs. Keckley finally appeared, however, and once Mary saw herself arrayed in that becoming bright rose color, with pearl necklace, earrings, and bracelets, and with red roses in her hair, she was in a happy mood again. Especially as just then Mr. Lincoln came in dressed in his long-tailed evening clothes and remarked to her as he pulled on his gloves, "I declare, you look charming in that dress."

He offered her his arm and with smiling face and queenly bearing Mary started with her husband down the stairs. As always, her spirits rose for a party. She undoubtedly enjoyed that ceremonial descent of President and First Lady into the festive scene below.

Then she and Mr. Lincoln stood shaking hands with a line of people which seemed endless. By and by Mary found out what all people in public life discover, that prolonged handshaking makes your hand sore and painful. Plucky as she was, she had to drop back and give up constant handshaking. Mr. Lincoln continued to shake hands steadily for two and a half hours and at the end of the ordeal he said his hand was so swollen he could not sign his name.

Yet no sign of this discomfort must appear in the faces of the President and First Lady. They must greet each person with a look of pleasure and say an appropriate word or two.

Mary did her part well. If Madame Mentelle on these occasions could have watched her former pupil to whom she had taught "graces and manners," she would have been very proud. There was more to Mary's attitude, however, than mere etiquette. She liked people and was interested in them. In that snobbish age it was noticed that she was "equally gracious to all," no matter how poorly they were dressed.

Except for one dark interruption these receptions were to go on for four years. You can get a close-up look at the Lincolns receiving their guests through the eyes of a newspaperwoman named Jane Swisshelm who was present at a reception about two years later. Jane was a fiery little woman known for her writings against slavery. When she told about this event, she explained she had not wanted to come to the reception at all because she was sure she would not like President Lincoln and his wife. Friends brought her under protest, and just to show her contempt for the whole occasion, she wore her old

Festivity at the White House

This lithograph is a composite picture of two receptions given by the Lincolns. It is an accurate drawing of the great East Room, but it has portraits of notable people who were at the different receptions. President Lincoln and Mary are shaking hands with Mrs. Grant, whose husband, General Grant, stands back of her. Nearby are Vice President Johnson, Chief Justice Chase, Secretary Stanton, Chase's daughter Kate, and Secretary Seward.

clothes and kept her coat over her arm. She scorned getting into the line to meet them but stood aside with hostile face to watch them greeting the crowd.

As she studied the Presidential pair, her unfriendly expression began to change. She found Mr. Lincoln's "sad, earnest, honest face was irresistible," she said, and "Mrs. Lincoln's manner was so simple and motherly" that Jane promptly got herself into line to meet them. Jane was an experienced person and she knew what an ordeal that endless handshaking was, so when Mr. Lincoln took her hand she burst out impulsively: "May the Lord have mercy on you, poor man, for the people have none." Mr. Lincoln laughed heartily. When Jane came to Mrs. Lincoln, the First Lady did not catch her name at first and asked to hear it again, and then, as Jane told it, "a sudden glow of pleasure lit her face, as she held out her hand, and said how very glad she was to see me." Jane was sorry then she had worn her old things and she said she was afraid her black glove would soil Mrs. Lincoln's white one. But Mary answered, "Then I shall preserve the glove to remember a great pleasure, for I have long wished to meet you." She knew of Jane's writing against slavery and Mary, like her husband, passionately believed in setting the slaves free.

A newspaperman who had watched Washington affairs for a long time summed up Mary's performance as hostess. Not since the time of the tactful and charming Dolly Madison, he said, had the White House "been graced by a lady as well fitted by nature and by education to dispense its hospitalities as is Mrs. Lincoln." Realizing that her way of meeting people came from a warm and sympathetic personality, he added, "Her hospitality is only equalled by her charity, and her graceful deportment by her goodness of heart."

In preparation for all the required entertainment Mary, soon after she went to the White House, made the first of her trips to New York to shop for its new furnishings. By this time she had learned something which she found hard to take: many of the high society people of Washington looked down on persons from Illinois as positively "uncivilized." She felt these snobbish individuals believed that she did not know how to select appropriate furnishings. Others, seeking her favor, offered Mary advice, telling her, "They say you are a Western woman, and that brilliant life is unknown to you. Prove by your style and splendor that to be Western is not to be a boor."

Mary never needed any encouragement to be extravagant. With salesmen outdoing themselves in showing her lovely, costly objects, she bought lavishly and, in the end, having beautiful taste, she made the interior of the White House a model of magnificence. The gold and purple draperies she selected for a bedroom were worthy of royalty. The carpet for the East Room was described as the "most exquisite" it had ever had. It was a pale green velvet and gave the effect as if the ocean, "in gleaming and transparent waves, were tossing roses at your feet." But she spent more money than Congress had set aside for the purpose and an additional appropriation had to be passed.

This brought a flood of criticism, over which Mary shed many bitter tears. Her intentions had been of the best in all those tiring trips she had taken to the New York stores. By the time the refurbishing was complete, however, a tragic change had come to Washington. People who had said Mrs. Lincoln was not a proper person to select the things were now saying that she should not have spent the money on such luxuries at all. For by this time the nation had plunged into its great Civil War.

The war had begun the middle of April, when the Lincolns had been in the White House less than a month and a half. The nation had divided against itself into North and South and President Lincoln's great task was to save it from its fall.

Civil war is a catastrophe like a huge tornado or flood which sweeps over a land wrecking homes, killing people and leaving misery in its wake. It does more than storm or flood, it sets friend against friend, brother against brother, and destroys the normal kindliness and goodwill of people, creating instead fear, suspicion and hate. Fate had placed Mary with her husband at the very storm center of our nation's great tragedy.

No woman could have been in a more difficult and lonely position than she was. It was no longer merely a question of Washington society tilting its nose at her; now the whole country was against her. The Southerners despised her, the wife of the Union President, as a traitor to her own people. Northerners learning that her brothers were in the Southern army were suspicious of her loyalty and rumors flew around that she was a Confederate spy. The reason Jane Swisshelm gave for not wanting to meet Mrs. Lincoln was that she thought her a spy and a woman who believed in slavery. The terrible gossip and accusations increased as war more and more darkened the land. Had Mary been perfect, which no human being ever is, the criticism would have been the same.

With the outbreak of war, Washington changed overnight into a city of fear. It was open to attack until soldiers could come from the North to protect it. The White House was filled with guards for the emergency, guards who even camped in the great East Room. Outside in the deserted streets public buildings were barricaded and protected by sentinels. The city was holding its breath in fear of invasion by the Confederates and praying that the Union soldiers would soon arrive. The strain went on for more than a week and even President Lincoln, looking out of the window in the direction from which help was expected, said in a low, desperate voice, "Why don't they come! Why don't they come!"

When a New York regiment arrived on April 25 and marched along Pennsylvania Avenue with band playing and flags flying, the President stood in front of the White House to welcome them. Mary was also there, hollow-eyed from worry and sleeplessness, and she wept with relief to see the strong young soldiers march by. With her were Willie and Tad, both much excited and each wearing one of the new Union badges to show what a stanch Unionist he was.

One event after another drove home to Mary the awfulness of civil war. Her affection for her relatives was strong, yet one brother and three half brothers were going into the Confederate army. Oh if only Emilie, the "Little Sister" who was so dear to Mr. Lincoln and herself, would be on their side! President Lincoln offered Emilie's husband, Ben Hardin Helm, a wonderful position in the Union army. This would have brought the young couple to Washington and Mary longed for Emilie in the loneliness of her high station.

But Ben Hardin Helm, like Robert E. Lee, could not bring his conscience to fighting against his native South. He declined the position and went into the Confederate army. It was terrible to Mary to realize that Emilie and Ben, whom she and Mr. Lincoln both loved, were now their enemies.

In the latter part of May a young man named Elmer Ellsworth, whom they had known in Springfield and brought with them on that long, roundabout journey to Washington, was killed. They had loved him almost like a son. On that dark day when the news of his death filled the Lincolns with horror, the President could not hear Ellsworth's name mentioned without giving way to tears. At the young officer's funeral, which was held in the East Room of the White House, Mary was completely unable to control her grief.

Then, early on the morning of July 21, a strange, ominous sound was heard in the distance. Willie asked his father what it was and reported in great excitement, "Pa says there's a battle in Virginia; that's big cannons going off that sounds like slamming doors." It was the battle of Bull Run. Nerves in the White House were always strained to the breaking point during battles and a visitor remembered how convulsively Mary's hands would jerk at each distant report that meant fighting and killing was going on south of them.

At first the news from the battle was that the Union soldiers were winning. But suddenly a telegram came saying the battle was lost and it was a question now of saving Washington and what was left of the Union army. Panic seized the city with the belief that it would be bombarded and captured. General Winfield Scott insisted that Mrs. Lincoln and the children should be sent north at once. Mary turned her pale face to her husband and asked, "Will you go with us?" Mr. Lincoln answered quickly, "Most assuredly I will not leave at this juncture." Mary's reply was just as prompt, "Then I will not leave you at this juncture." Fortunately no attack on Washington followed.

Thus the nerve-racking months of the first year with their light and dark events moved on. Mary, though she enjoyed the importance and glamor of her new position, was often heartsick and homesick. How peaceful the neighborly years in Springfield now seemed. Occasionally one of the relatives or old friends from Illinois would come to Washington and be cordially welcomed. But midwinter brought a visitor from Springfield who was the last person Mary would have chosen to come, William Herndon, her husband's junior law partner. He came to ask a favor of the President, who welcomed him kindly and loaned him twenty-five dollars to get home when he ran out of money.

Mary, who neither liked nor approved of Herndon, was certainly not pleased to have him turn up like this. Whether she saw Herndon on this visit is not clear, but he evidently picked up some of the abusive stories which were circulating about her, because when he went home he wrote a friend that Mrs. Lincoln was a "wicked woman."

Three years later Herndon, through a friend, asked President Lincoln for an appointment, "any large, honorable, & fat office with a big salary." He did not receive the appointment and there was talk in Springfield that Mary had influenced her husband not to give it to him. With Mr. Lincoln knowing that Herndon's drinking habits and lack of balanced judgment made him unfit for such an office, it is doubtful whether any wifely influence was necessary. But Herndon evidently believed that Mrs. Lincoln had worked against him and he was storing up a mighty resentment against her, a hatred that was to lash out in deadly fury in the future. It was so much easier to blame her than to face up to the fact that his own qualities were largely responsible for his failure to rise in the world.

The receptions and dinners continued to go on with their pomp and circumstance. Mary was roundly abused for having these elaborate social occasions when the country was at war. She would have been equally abused for not doing her duty if she had discontinued them.

When a royal visitor came to the United States, it was proper for the President to entertain him. Such a visitor was the French Prince Napoleon, who reached Washington that first summer and was honored with a large formal dinner at the White House. The Marine Band on the lawn outside was just finishing its Saturday concert for the people when the prince arrived and he was invited to step out on the south balcony of the White House to see and be seen by the crowd. It was a high moment of drama for Mary when she stood beside the resplendent figure of the prince on that historic balcony. He wore many brilliant decorations and the crimson sash which crossed his princely breast seemed to add the final touch of glamor.

One can imagine the long gleaming table in the state dining room on that evening and Mary's skill at presiding as hostess. Few women could have talked with the prince in his own language as she did, thanks to Madame Mentelle's thorough teaching. It is easy to picture the look of pride on Mr. Lincoln's face as he heard her conversing fluently in a foreign tongue which he had never had a chance to learn.

Many people noticed the expression of the President's face as he gazed at Mary. A friend who was devoted to both of them once described it as "the *pleasing look* of *Abraham Lincoln* — for *her whom he so loved*." Another friend who was chatting with the President at one of the receptions in the East Room one evening suddenly noticed that his attention had wandered from what she was saying. His eyes were on Mary dressed in party best, and with her face lighted with friendliness. Realizing that he had been caught in the act, Mr. Lincoln laughed pleasantly and said, "My wife is as handsome as when she was a girl, and I, a poor nobody then, fell in love with her.

"And what is more," he continued, "I have never fallen out."

15

"We Loved Him So"

*T*HIS great single devotion which Abraham Lincoln gave her was the cornerstone of Mary's existence. The essential thing to her was to love and be loved by her husband and children. She found it fun in many ways to play her part as First Lady, but its glory vanished with the first hint of threat to them.

In Washington her most important role was still that of wife and mother. Since the White House was now their home, the center of it for "Father" and the boys was "Mother's room." It was here Mr. Lincoln would come for a few minutes of relaxation from his endless duties and problems. He would throw himself wearily on the sofa, read (often in the Bible which lay ready on a stand within arm's reach), or chat with Mary a little while before walking down the long hall to his office again.

Since Robert was away at Harvard the White House family, except during vacations, consisted only of father and mother and the two younger boys. "Mother's room"

Mary as First Lady

Mary felt that her pictures were not very satisfactory because, she said, "my hands are always *made* in *them*, very large and I look too stern." But Mr. Brady, photographer of the one to the right, managed to catch a bit of a smile.

was also where Willie and Tad came for aid and comfort when they could not think of anything more active to do. Willie, who loved books, liked to curl up near his mother and read. Mary's whole heart was given to this lovable son who was so exactly like his father. She dearly loved the unpredictable Taddie too, she called him her "little troublesome *sunshine*," but Willie was her child of greatest promise and her favorite. With her ever-underlying sense of insecurity, she often said that he "would be the hope and stay of her old age." Willie, handsome, bright, sensible, and sweet-tempered, was also the very idol of his father's heart.

Shortly after the Inauguration Mary, knowing how queer this new life in the White House seemed to the little boys, began to look around for some playmates for them. When she met a judge's wife, Mrs. Horatio Taft, and found out that she had two little sons called Bud and Holly who were about the ages of Willie and Tad, she said eagerly, "Send them around to-morrow, please, Mrs. Taft. Willie and Tad are so lonely and everything is so strange to them here in Washington."

Their sixteen-year-old sister Julia brought the Taft boys to the White House. Bud promptly became Willie's crony while Holly paired off with Tad, and for the rest of the year the four irrepressible little boys were constantly together, having a tumultuous and wonderful time. Julia was usually sent along with them with instructions to see that "those young rascals don't tear down the White House."

We have looked at Mary through many pairs of eyes in this story; now we can borrow the bright intelligent eyes of this young girl to gaze at her. Julia was shy, having been repressed by a mother who believed in the prevailing stern rules for rearing children, including the rule that they should be seen and not heard. Julia had been taught that "young girls were not supposed to have opinions" and "certainly not to air them in the presence of their elders." It often made her feel tongue-tied.

The first time Julia met Mrs. Lincoln she entered the room timidly, not knowing what to expect. She found herself being greeted warmly and she thought that Mrs. Lincoln, who "was dressed in a fresh lilac organdy," looked "very attractive." Mary seated the girl on the sofa beside her and began to ask her questions about herself with such genuine interest that suddenly Julia's shyness melted and she found she could talk. In no time at all she felt perfectly natural and was showing Mrs. Lincoln her new hat.

Julia Taft and Mrs. Lincoln quickly came to love each other and Julia would always remember how "sweet and tender" Mary was to her. "I wish I had a little girl like you, Julia," Mrs. Lincoln would often say, and then once she told Julia about her second son, who had died when he was still almost a baby and such a dear little fellow. The girl and the woman cried together over the sadness of little Eddie's death.

Julia told Mrs. Lincoln things she would never have dreamed of telling her own unapproachable mother. She opened her heart to Mary about the boy friend who had joined the Confederate army and thus became an enemy, and how this hurt. Mary with her own brothers fighting on the other side, said gently, "Yes, dear, it is sad when our friends are in the rebel army." Julia had taken music lessons and Mrs. Lincoln would often ask her to play. Julia hated to play for her critical parents, but when Mary stood by her at the piano turning the sheets of music, the girl found it pleasant to play for someone who was so understanding and sympathetic.

Julia had the thrill of her first long dress that year. It was not only long, it had a train to it and was low in the neck so that she was afraid it might slip off her shoulders. The small, slim girl with her smooth curls and fine young face must have looked very lovely in that dress when her father took her to a White House reception. They had to worm their way through the dense crowd to get in line, and when they were within a few steps of the President, someone spread out her train for her in all its glory. Just then a great big cavalryman fresh from one of the camps walked right over it and caught one of his spurs in the delicate fabric. It took quite a while to get that spur loose and Julia was in an agony of mortification at being tied by her train to the foot of a huge soldier. She was not helped by the fact that her father looked frightfully annoyed and people were smiling all around at the incident. But President and Mrs. Lincoln did not smile at her embarrassment; they greeted her as if nothing at all had happened and that was a great comfort.

Afterwards Mary made her feel better about it by praising her for carrying it off so well.

Much as Julia loved Mrs. Lincoln, she felt, like the people at Springfield, that the Lincolns spoiled their children. Willie and Tad with Bud and Holly Taft were practically turning the White House upside down, but whatever they did, Mrs. Lincoln would smile and say, "Let the children have a good time." The catch for Julia was that she had to look after them while they were doing it.

She was quite disgusted one day when the four boys decided to have a circus in the attic. Mrs. Lincoln let Willie and Bud have two of her dresses and one of her bonnets so that they could dress up as lovely ladies. Julia had to pin up Mrs. Lincoln's lilac silk (with low neck and long train) around Willie and her "white morning dress" on Bud, whose appearance had an added touch of the ridiculous because he had put the lady's bonnet on sideways. Julia straightened it, blacked Tad's face with burnt cork for his part, and then left, refusing to attend the performance. The President of the United States, however, did attend, paying five cents admission at the door and getting lots of fun out of the boys' antics and singing.

Such games of the romping little boys seemed the only thing in the White House that was normal and happy after the war started. Everything had soon taken on a military aspect. Camps sprang up all around Washington and it was one of Mary's duties which she liked very much to visit these camps, usually taking Willie and Tad along with her. It cheered the soldiers, who were home-sick for their wives and children, to have the President's family come bringing choice food, flowers, books, and other things not found in military camps. The soldiers liked Mrs. Lincoln with her interest, sympathy, and lack of pretense and they decided to name one of the camps for her.

Mary with a small party rode out in a handsome car-riage for the christening of the camp. She wore a beauti-ful silk bonnet sent to her from Massachusetts, a patriotic bonnet with the Stars and Stripes woven into its design. The regiment stood in line before the carriage while the colonel made a stirring patriotic speech. Then he lifted a bottle of champagne and broke it on the carriage wheel, christening the tented field Camp Mary Lincoln. The regiment broke into uproarious cheers "for the President, for his accomplished lady, and for the Union." It was all very thrilling, and after that Willie and Tad were al-ways wanting to take something nice to the soldiers at "Mother's" camp.

The milestone of New Year's Day came bringing in the year 1862. Early in February the Lincolns were to give an elaborate reception and invitations were sent out well in advance. Then one day Willie was taken sick. His face was flushed with fever and Mary's heart sank, as it always did when one of her children was ill. She wanted to cancel the invitations, but the doctor said Willie was getting along all right and to go ahead with the plans.

When February 5, the day of the party arrived, Willie grew suddenly worse.

That reception was a nightmare to Mary. In the East Room bright lights fell from the glittering chandeliers on the brilliant scene and costly costumes, the Marine Band played gay music, people laughed and talked. The great parlor was gorgeous with decorations; the refreshment tables were adorned with masterpieces of confectionery on patriotic themes. One of the most striking of these was a big cake or candy model of a ship labeled *Union* complete with flying Stars and Stripes.

Five hundred people came to the reception. Mary, dressed in white satin trimmed with black lace, had to stand greeting the endless blur of faces, while all the time her mind was upstairs in the room with gold and purple hangings where Willie lay burning with fever. Mrs. Keckley was watching over him, but several times Mary slipped away to go up and see him. She would lay her hand gently on the hot little forehead or stroke his hair, her heart torn with anxiety and love. When she would return to the East Room, her husband's eyes would catch hers with a mute question to which she could give back no reassurance.

The illness dragged on for days. Sometimes Willie seemed better, sometimes worse. On his father's birthday, February 12, he was reported out of danger, which made the best of birthday presents. But five days later the doctors told the father and mother the cruel truth that the boy could not get well. After that Mary stayed almost constantly at his bedside. As darkness settled down over the White House on the evening of February 20, Willie fell asleep for the last time.

The parents were crushed with grief. Even while Mr. Lincoln tried to accept Willie's death as God's will, he cried out in his agony, "but then we loved him so." Mary, worn out from her long nursing, lay ill. Sometimes she was quiet from exhaustion, then she would go into strange spasms of weeping and crying. This sorrow was too great for one of her unsteady nerves and temperament; she could not go through it unimpaired.

Mary had not come to the White House in good health, though she had carried on bravely in spite of this as a plucky person will. She was still having the migraine headaches which would make her wretchedly ill. Then, like many people in that age when doctors had little medical knowledge with which to fight disease, she suffered from recurring attacks of ague, a kind of malaria which would lay her low for days with chills and fever. She had other ailments that were not in sight, to weaken her and give her pain.

Fate had now darkened the stage for the drama of Mary Lincoln's story. Some gifted writer might have found her life the challenging subject for a famous play, so strange and dramatic it was, and so tied up with history. The fundamental theme of that play would have been, as in so many dramas, a great love. But it also would have been a Shakespearean tragedy. One of the most poignant elements of that tragedy was now to appear.

A hidden trouble of Mary's had made its ominous beginning. Mr. Lincoln, out of his deep love for his wife and out of his understanding of people's minds and hearts, had recognized it. There was something abnormal in her wild paroxysms of grief. One day when she was beside herself in one of her emotional outbursts, he took her arm and gently drew her to a window. Pointing to a house where people who were mentally ill were kept, he said, "Mother, do you see that large white building on the hill yonder? Try and control your grief, or it will drive you mad, and we may have to send you there."

In Springfield he had known that her hysterical seizures or "nervous spells," as he called them, had come from not being well. Now his words showed that he suspected the dreadful truth, that mental illness was threatened or already involved for the wife he so dearly loved.

There was nothing he could do except to be even more tender and patient, as he would have done if she had become lame or blind. Even less was known at that time about the ailments of the mind than about those of the body. There was no psychiatrist, no competent specialist in mental diseases, from whom he could get help for Mary. Mental illness was considered something of a disgrace and people who were thus innocently ill were called "lunatics."

Only those close to her realized that in one respect

Mary was becoming irrational. As an infection often settles in one spot, in a hand, a foot, or elsewhere in a body otherwise sound, so her mental illness was located around one subject. She was increasingly obsessed with the belief that she and her husband were very poor and on the verge of being in want. It was an idea that came from her sense of insecurity, which had grown greater than ever under the forces beating against her in the White House. Along with her obsession that they were poor went an urge for extravagant buying, a strange combination but one which specialists in mental illnesses often find. It was not possible for her to think straight about her extravagance and supposed poverty, yet in other matters she was normal and keenly intelligent.

For ten days after Willie's death Mary was prostrate in bed. Slowly a measure of physical strength returned and her hysteria became less frequent. Two things helped her to take up her life again. The strongest was her husband's great need of her in his own overwhelming sorrow about Willie's death. "If I had not felt the spur of necessity urging me to cheer Mr. Lincoln, whose grief was as great as my own," she told her sister Emilie later, "I could never have smiled again." His sad, stricken face aroused all her loving instinct to help and protect him. She would use all kinds of wifely devices to coax him to eat and would beg him to take her riding, so that he would get a bit of rest from his heavy duties.

Taddie, lost and sad without Willie, needed her too. Bud and Holly soon went North to school and Tad became the constant companion of his father and mother. He was an affectionate, sympathetic little fellow and in his nine-year-old way he tried to cheer his parents and show his love for them.

Mary rallied for the sake of her husband and her two remaining sons. The second thing that comforted her was that by June she had found a way to help the sons of other mothers, the wounded soldiers lying in the hospitals in Washington. She began to make almost daily visits to them, passing between the long rows of cots, giving them fruit or dainty food and words of tender sympathy. Some of the pale faces on the pillows were pitifully young and it tore at her heart to see how cruelly they were hurt, but pain-filled eyes would brighten as she stood beside them and she felt she had helped a little.

For the rest of the year she could not face having receptions and other White House entertainments. Of course there were many who roundly criticized her for omitting them. She would never again enter the bedroom with the gold and purple hangings where Willie had died, or the Green Room where he had lain in his coffin. She knew if she did she could not control her emotions.

She seemed almost to hate the White House, toward which she had looked longingly for so many years. The first of July the Lincolns moved out to Soldiers' Home, a house about two and a half miles out of Washington where they could live more quietly for the rest of the summer. It meant so much to get away from the crowds which filled the White House. But the move to this summer home required Mr. Lincoln to ride back and forth each morning and evening. One August night as he was returning to Soldiers' Home, a shot rang out in the darkness and a bullet went through his hat. After that Mary's fear of his being assassinated grew sharper than ever. She would beg him never to go out alone, but no fearless man likes to have guards tagging along with him and he would answer, "What does anyone want to harm me for? Don't worry about me, Mother, as if I were a little child, for no one is going to molest me." But she could not help worrying.

So the dark year of 1862 drew to its close. Mary had passed, as she said, "through the fiery furnace of affliction."

16

Divided Family
in a Divided Nation

*W*HEN the year 1863 came in Mary had recovered suffi-
ciently to resume her role as White House hostess. Having been widely criticized for not giving the usual entertainments, she felt it was her duty. "My position," she
said, "requires my presence, where my heart, is *so far*
from being." She and the President gave a huge reception on New Year's Day and their hearts had reason to
be uplifted as they received their guests. January 1, 1863,
was the day on which Mr. Lincoln issued his famous
Emancipation Proclamation which freed the slaves.

A great exultation swept over Mary. No more slavery!
No more would it be possible for evil masters to inflict
the horrible things which had so shocked her and Elizabeth Humphreys when they were little girls. No more
would dear people like Mammy Sally and Old Nelson be
exposed to the chance of getting into the hands of a cruel
master. And it was her husband who had brought about

this blessing, this end to what she called "the great evil, that has been so long allowed, to curse the land. The decree," she continued, "has gone forth, that 'all men are free'. . . . It is a rich & precious legacy, for my sons & one for which, I am sure, and *believe*, they will always bless God & their father."

On February 13, the day after Mr. Lincoln's birthday, another reception took place in the East Room. This one, however, was different. Gentlemen in long-tailed coats and ladies in gorgeous gowns stood about in groups, as usual, but they had an air of excited expectancy. It was as if the crowd was waiting for a show to begin.

Suddenly from the doorway came a loud announcement of the guests of honor. Down the long parlor came two doll-like figures, a perfect little man about three feet in height dressed in an elegant miniature wedding suit, and a pretty little lady slightly shorter than he who was clad in a white satin wedding dress trimmed with point lace, orange blossoms, and pearls. Behind her spreading hoop skirt was a train about twice as long as she was. The two walked forward toward President and Mrs. Lincoln with "pigeon-like stateliness."

They were famous midgets whose real names were Mr. and Mrs. Charles Sherwood Stratton, but the public knew them as General and Mrs. Tom Thumb. They had been married three days before in New York, and people were so taken with the wee couple that accounts of their elaborate wedding had almost pushed the war news off the first pages of the newspapers. Then they

Famous Midgets

The well-known midgets General and Mrs. Tom Thumb (their real names were Mr. and Mrs. Charles Stratton) were entertained at a White House reception. Tad said to Mrs. Lincoln, "Mother, if you were a little woman like Mrs. Stratton you would look just like her."

had come to Washington and Mary was giving a reception for them.

When the pigmy pair stood before the Lincolns, the other guests must have found it hard not to smile at the contrast between the tall President and the little general. Mr. Lincoln, his rugged face very kind, bent down and shook the tiny hands in turn. Both he and Mary were careful to treat the midgets as if they were as normal in size as anyone else.

Tad was present on this unusual occasion. He was nearly ten now, and when he stood beside the petite couple he was suddenly impressed with how wonderfully tall he was. Tad had grown less harum-scarum and it was becoming clear that he had a very tender heart. He wanted to take good care of these fascinating little people. When Mary began arranging for them to have their refreshments off a chair, he helped to make them comfortable with an air of protectiveness.

Tad's keen eyes had noted an extraordinary fact. Later the little bride herself told what happened. The President, she said, "took our hands and led us to the sofa, lifting the General up and placed him at his left hand, while Mrs. Lincoln did the same service for me, placing me at her right. . . . Tad, the favorite son, stood beside his mother and gazing at me . . . whispered to his mother, 'Mother if you were a little woman like Mrs. Stratton you would look just like her.'" People around were noticing this too and staring in amazement. The shape of Mrs. Thumb's face and the lines of her figure were like Mrs. Lincoln's in miniature. It seemed Mary's destiny to have unusual things happen to her. What other First Lady ever stood in the festive East Room gazing down on a tiny living, breathing replica of herself?

That year was full of out-of-the-way events. When the evening of April 4, Tad's birthday, arrived, no one would have expected to find him and his parents in the place where they were: that is, on board the President's steamboat, the *Carrie Martin*, which was anchored in an inlet on the Potomac River in a blinding snowstorm. If the Confederates had known about it, they might have made a raid on the Potomac that night and have captured the President of the United States! The Presidential family was on its way to visit the headquarters of the Union army in Virginia and the unexpected, furious snowing had forced the steamboat to tie up to the bank.

Mary, seeing how worn out her husband was and knowing that neither of them could ever relax in the White House, had suggested the trip. President Lincoln was also commander in chief of the Union army and she said truly that it greatly cheered the soldiers to have him visit their camps. She needed all her good sportsmanship on that journey. The snow was still falling when they landed, and next they had to ride on a freight car fitted up with rough plank benches. During their visit they slept on camp bedsteads in tents.

But the days were filled with excitement, color, and

pageantry. In front of the President in the reviewing stand marched a vast array of soldiers. Blue-uniformed columns on foot and cavalrymen on their prancing horses paraded by, to the crash of band music and the waving of the Stars and Stripes. It made Mary's heart beat fast to look at them.

She and Mr. Lincoln were driven around the encampments. Once they came to a queer little settlement of Negro refugees. The people flocked eagerly out of their shanties, their brown faces shining with joyous excitement as they shouted, "Hurrah for Massa Linkum." Mary looked with warm friendliness at the little colored children and gaily asked her husband how many of them, did he suppose, were named Abraham Lincoln. "Let's see," he answered, "this is April, 1863. I should say that of all those babies under two years of age, perhaps two thirds have been named for me."

When summer came the Lincolns again moved out to Soldiers' Home. On July 1, all nerves began to tighten in Washington at the news that a great battle was beginning at Gettysburg, Pennsylvania. The next morning Mary got into the Presidential carriage to drive into the city. Unknown to anyone, hostile hands had been at that carriage with the intention to kill or cripple President Lincoln. The screws which held the driver's seat in place had been removed. Shortly after the carriage started, the seat came loose, throwing the driver out, and the frightened horses ran away. Mary, alone in the carriage, was hurled violently to the ground, where the back of her head — that head which had already known so much agonizing pain — struck a sharp rock. She was carried to a hospital where her wounds were dressed and then she was taken back to Soldiers' Home.

But the wound became badly infected and for days she lay dangerously ill. The care of a faithful nurse finally brought her through to recovery. Mr. Lincoln, his eyes haggard with his long anxiety, was almost pathetic in his gratitude to this nurse for saving "Mother's life." The accident, however, was another heavy blow to Mary's sick nerves. Two years later her son Robert was to say, "I think mother has never quite recovered from the effects of her fall." Then, in this connection, Robert spoke of her pluck: "It is really astonishing what a brave front she manages to keep when we know she is suffering — most women would be in bed groaning, but not mother!" Yet Mary's feeling of insecurity was increased by the happening and Mr. Lincoln was further pulled down by those days and nights of worry about her. He was already under terrible strain about the battle of Gettysburg when the accident occurred.

There seemed to be no such thing as rest or peace for either of them. She had thought up the April visit to the army to take him from the tension in the White House, but he had said to her on that trip, "It is a great relief to get away from Washington and the politicians. But nothing touches the tired spot." Nothing could reach Mary's tired spot either.

As soon as she was able to travel after the accident she

went (or was sent) on a trip North. Doctors then (probably because they did not know anything else to do) were in the habit of sending sick people on journeys as a cure. For various reasons Mary was going on frequent trips now, sometimes to lend the presence of the First Lady at some public function, sometimes to shop or visit her son Robert at Harvard, but most of all, one suspects, to get away from that whirling storm center, the White House.

As with all devoted couples, she and her husband, when apart, wanted to keep in close touch with each other. They exchanged telegrams constantly, often more than one a day. Brief as the telegrams were, they show fully the deep love and concern between the two. With hundreds of details to look after, the President was still taking thought for Mary's comfort when he wired her, "Do not come on the night train. It is too cold. Come in the morning." Each, with the unselfishness which goes with great love, wished to conceal from the other anything that would cause worry. Mr. Lincoln always dutifully telegraphed her that he was well but, knowing he did not want her to be uneasy, once she checked on him by wiring Old Edward, the faithful doorman at the White House, "Let me know immediately exactly how Mr. Lincoln and Taddie are."

It was intensely hot in Washington that summer and Mary was one of those people who could not stand extreme heat. In August she was forced to go North, where she stayed at the Tip Top House on Mount

Washington. A newspaperman chatted with her while she was there and was much taken with her "easy, agreeable way" and pleasing appearance. Mrs. Lincoln, he wrote, "has a very fair, cheerful, smiling face, which does one good to look upon." Her hair was so rich in color he called it "dark auburn."

Slowly the heat of summer passed into the coolness of fall. Always in the background of daily thought and living was the Civil War with bloody battles that brought alternate victory or defeat. The Union forces had been victorious at the battle of Gettysburg in July and it had been decided to set aside a portion of the great battlefield for a soldiers' cemetery. The President was asked to make a short speech at the dedication of this cemetery on November 19.

Mr. Lincoln liked to have Mary go places with him, but this time she could not do it because Tad was ill. She stayed at the White House to take care of him and report his condition to his anxious father. Her first telegram to Mr. Lincoln after he departed to Pennsylvania brought a bit of reassurance: "The Dr. has just left. We hope dear Taddie is slightly better. Will send you a telegram in the morning." Mary missed hearing the immortal words of the President on the battlefield of Gettysburg that day, where again he spoke of the "great task" of saving the Union from the dividing which would lead to its fall.

When he returned Tad was better but he himself was feeling ill. He was coming down with varioloid, a mild form of smallpox. To have Mr. Lincoln ill made Mary feel that she had lost her last prop.

The Civil War was now in its third year. The longer it lasted the more intense grew bitterness, suspicion, and hate. Mr. Lincoln's political enemies were constantly hurling criticisms and accusations at him. If they could tear down the reputation of his wife, that would injure him indirectly, so Mary also was more and more the target of malicious slander. She was accused of almost everything inflamed imaginations could think of, but because she had brothers fighting on the Confederate side, the favorite accusation was that she was a traitor to the Union and a spy.

The April after Willie's death her half brother Sam Todd had been killed in battle fighting for the South. He was the one who in happier days had playfully taught her son Bobbie to call him "Uncle Sam." Then, several months after his death, his brother Alec had likewise been killed — Alec, the dear little red-headed fellow who such a few years before had played and romped with Bobbie when they visited Lexington. He had clung to her so lovingly that when she put one arm around Bobbie she must needs put the other arm around him too.

Mary's affectionate heart could not help but grieve for these lost brothers. Yet in the days following the news about them, suspicious eyes kept watching her face for signs of grieving. She must, against her own family loyalty, pretend that she did not care and remember only, as she said, that "they would kill my husband if they could, and destroy our Government — the dearest of all things to us."

She was keenly sensitive to the false and terrible stories circulated about her but she had learned there were worse troubles than slander. "I know it seems hard that I should be maligned," she said to a sympathetic and indignant friend, "and I used to shed many bitter tears about it, but since I have known real sorrow — since little Willie died, — all these shafts have no power to wound me. If I could lay my head on my pillow at night, and feel that I had wronged no one, that is all I have wished since his death."

In the fall of 1863 news came of another Confederate death which caused the Lincolns deep grief. Ben Hardin Helm, the husband of Emilie, was killed in battle in September. Mary's heart went out to the beloved "Little Sister" who was left in desperate circumstances in the deep South with three tiny children. Emilie wanted to get back to her mother in Lexington, Kentucky, but arranging to go through the lines into Union territory was slow and difficult. Finally in December she started with her little daughter Katherine. When she reached Fort Monroe the Federal officers there told her she could not go farther unless she took an oath of allegiance to the United States.

One of the most tragic things about the Civil War was that people on each side were fighting for what they sincerely believed was right. Emilie's allegiance was given

"*Little Sister*" *Grown Up and Married*

Emilie with her husband, Ben Hardin Helm, before the war. Mary wrote to her from Springfield: "If you do not bring yourself & Husband to see us very soon, we will think you are not as proud of *Him* as rumor says you should be." Emilie's smile indicates she is as proud of "*Him*" as any rumor could wish.

to the Confederacy. Her husband had died fighting under the Confederate flag and she felt that she would be a traitor if she took the oath of allegiance to the Union. She refused to do so. The officers found out they were holding the sister-in-law of their President and wired him asking what to do. Back came the brief but dramatic reply, "Send her to me." So Emilie, a stanch Confederate and therefore one of the enemy, was brought to the White House.

When they greeted her it was hard for Mary and Mr. Lincoln to connect this pale, black-clad widow with the glowing young girl for whom in Springfield they had once bought the white velvet bonnet with lovely nodding plumes. They put their arms around her, held her close, and for a moment all were too choked up with tears to speak. Loving caresses were safer than words when their loyalties were so divided. They could not talk of the battles when for Mary a Union victory meant hope and for Emilie it meant despair. Mary felt deep pity for her younger sister in the loss of her husband, but how could she mention Ben's death when he had died fighting against all that Mr. Lincoln was fighting for. Emilie wrote in her diary, "This frightful war comes between us like a barrier of granite closing our lips but not our hearts . . ."

The softhearted Lincolns did everything they could to show their love. Once the older sister, to divert Emilie, took her for a drive in the Presidential carriage, and with the usual ill fortune that seemed to pursue Mary, the carriage ran over a little boy, breaking his leg. Mary, distressed beyond words, jumped out crying, "Oh, the poor baby! Who is he, where does he live? I will take him to his mother." She wanted to gather him up in her arms, but fortunately a doctor took charge of the boy and removed him to his home. Mary went at once to tell the mother how sorry she was about the accident and to assure her she would help in every way possible. In the days that followed the little invalid was showered with playthings, fruit, and flowers from the White House.

Emilie with little Katherine stayed with the Lincolns some days before Mr. Lincoln arranged for them to go on to Lexington. During her visit she noticed constantly the strain her older sister was under and what a change it had made in her. Once Emilie entered a room where Mary was reading a newspaper which, as often happened, contained slurs and accusations against her. She dropped the paper, held out her arms, and said despairingly, "Kiss me, Emilie, and tell me that you love me! I seem to be the scape-goat for both North and South!" Just then they heard Mr. Lincoln's voice as he approached and instantly Mary threw off her despondent expression and lifted her shoulders. She tried to be cheerful before him, for he was carrying a heavy load too and was still weak from his illness.

Emilie saw the mutual worry and the brave, pitiful attempts of these two to shield each other. Mary asked her anxiously, "Emilie, what do you think of Mr. Lincoln, do you think he is well?" Emilie thought to herself that he looked very ill but she merely answered, "He seems thinner than I ever saw him." "Oh, Emilie," exclaimed Mary, "will we ever awake from this hideous nightmare?"

When his wife was not present Mr. Lincoln confided to Emilie his anxiety about her. "I feel worried about Mary," he said, "her nerves have gone to pieces; she cannot hide from me that the strain she has been under has been too much for her mental as well as her physical health." In his turn he asked, "What do you think?" — perhaps hoping for a word of reassurance.

But Emilie too felt that a degree of mental illness had come to Mary and she answered guardedly, "She seems very nervous and excitable and once or twice when I have come into the room suddenly the frightened look in her eyes has appalled me."

Mr. Lincoln shook his head sadly. "Stay with her as long as you can," he said.

Emilie's presence started a fresh flood of criticism. Tongues were wagging furiously about the White House harboring one of the enemy. The sisters felt keenly that "barrier of granite" between them. In spite of family loyalty and affection, each thought the other a traitor to the cause that was right and patriotic.

Divided loyalties even made trouble between Tad and his little cousin Katherine Helm. The two children were sitting on a rug in front of the fire one day looking at photographs. Tad, holding up a picture of his father, said proudly, "This is the President." Small Katherine, like her mother, was loyal to Jefferson Davis, President of the Confederacy, so she shook her head violently and answered, "No, that is not the President, Mr. Davis is President." Tad was outraged and shouted, "Hurrah for Abe Lincoln." Katherine promptly yelled back, "Hurrah for Jeff Davis." At this point Mr. Lincoln, with twinkling eyes, drew the two glaring antagonists into his lap, one on each knee, and showed what a statesman he was by saying, "Well, Tad, you know who is your President, and I am your little cousin's Uncle Lincoln."

17

"His Dream Was Prophetic"

*T*HE year 1864 opened in the usual way with a huge New Year's reception at the White House. As if things were not already complicated enough, this had to be election year and it was a serious question whether Mr. Lincoln would be elected President for a second term. Mary was more than ready now to do a great deal of entertaining because she wanted to do her part socially to help his chances. She cheerfully remarked to a young man who was helping her arrange a party that she would do her duty no matter how much her guests pulled her to pieces with their criticisms.

Mr. Lincoln, overworked and worried, was doubtful whether he would be re-elected. He had another illness in February and Mary could not persuade him to eat enough. How could she tempt his appetite?

She had a sudden idea. She remembered his favorite dish in those happy days back home in Springfield. "Alice," she said to a young woman who was employed at the White House, "do you know how to make a dish of fricasseed chicken and small biscuits with thick cream gravy poured over it, all on one platter?"

"I'll try," replied Alice, entering wholeheartedly into the plan. "It would be so good to see Mr. Lincoln eat something."

They worked out the details with great care. They would have dinner in the small dining room with no servants present. Tad was the only one who could be depended on to fetch his father — the President would have told anyone else he was too busy to eat.

When Mr. Lincoln entered the room with Tad and saw the homelike setup and the steaming platter, he exclaimed, "Oh, Mary, this is good. It seems like old times come back!" There was something in the worn face and homesick voice that brought tears to Alice's eyes as she left the room. When she returned, she heard Mr. Lincoln laughing and Tad cried out joyfully, "Oh, Alice, he ate three helps and more gravy than you and me and mother could [together]!"

Bitter fighting continued throughout this year. The war-weary people were longing for some sign that it would end. In Washington now they could look to the skyline above the Capitol and see the finished dome curving upward to its apex, complete and beautiful. As long as it had been unfinished, it had been suggestive of the broken Union. In May the statue of Armed Freedom which crowned it was ceremoniously unveiled. As the fastenings were pulled away, a white dove circled the mighty head against the sky and then alighted upon it. An awed whisper went through the crowd, "a sign of peace." It was both a hope and a prayer.

Mary had frequent migraine headaches and other illnesses that spring and took a couple of trips North, perhaps to recover. She was in Washington, however, one day in July when again was heard that distant sound like the banging of giant doors which she knew now came from the firing of cannon. The fighting was at Fort Stevens, very close to Washington. Again the Confederates were near the capital.

The President considered it his duty to go out to Fort Stevens and she went along, probably because she refused to stay behind when he was running a risk. Mr. Lincoln stood up on the rampart in full view and Mary stood right beside him. If he was in danger she was going to share it. And he was in danger; unknown to them a Confederate sharpshooter had hidden in the top of a house and was ready to shoot any Union person who appeared. Once when Mr. Lincoln was standing on the parapet, a man beside him suddenly crumpled up with a shot in his leg. Mary was terribly frightened and begged her husband to leave the fort, but he refused to do so until he was ready.

This incident was a great ordeal to Mary, but what really hurt her most was that the enemy got away. Her fighting blood was up. She later made a spirited remark about it to Mr. Stanton, the Secretary of War. After the crisis was over, he said to her one day, "Mrs. Lincoln,

I intend to have a full-length portrait of you painted, standing on the ramparts at Fort Stevens overlooking the fight."

"That is very well," Mary retorted, "and I can assure you of one thing, Mr. Secretary, if I had had a few *ladies* with me the Rebels would not have been permitted to get away as they did!"

The chances for Mr. Lincoln's re-election looked especially dark that summer and Mary was almost frantic with anxiety. She had a new and secret worry; her obsession about being poor and the urge to extravagant buying had woven a snare about her. She had been purchasing more and more expensive dresses, furs, and jewels and charging them at the stores. The only one she had to confide in was Mrs. Keckley, the Negro seamstress, who by now had become a maid and companion to her. "I must dress in costly materials," she said to Mrs. Keckley. "The people scrutinize every article that I wear with critical curiosity."

Mary wept hysterically as she explained to Mrs. Keckley that she had run up large debts by her purchases and that Mr. Lincoln knew nothing about them. What if he should be defeated in the election and his salary as President would stop? Mary was sick in body and mind and her judgment was impaired, yet only a few who had been close to her, like her husband, Mrs. Keckley, and Emilie Helm, knew that in some ways she was not responsible for what she was doing.

Prospects for Mr. Lincoln's re-election began to

brighten by fall. When Election Day, November 8, finally came, it was as dark and stormy as the fears in Mary's heart. That evening when Mr. Lincoln went to the War Department to hear the election returns, she waited tensely in the White House, her nerves keyed up almost to the breaking point. When encouraging telegrams began to come, he promptly sent the news over to her, remarking to those around him, "She is more anxious than I." By midnight she could relax; it was clear that her husband had won the election and would be President for four more years.

The year 1865 opened with a whole series of entertainments. The newspapers outdid themselves in describing the First Lady's gowns as hostess: a "heavy brocade purple silk, very richly trimmed with black velvet, over which was thrown a rich and exquisitely wrought black lace shawl," or a "rich dress of pearl color, heavily trimmed with the richest black lace, with a neat headdress composed of a coronet of exquisite flowers." No wonder her debts were piling up.

By the first of March the sound of hammers was heard once more on the east front of the Capitol. The great platform was being built there to inaugurate Mr. Lincoln a second time. Inauguration Day, March 4, dawned dark and rainy. But at the moment in the ceremonies when Mr. Lincoln stepped forward to give his Inaugural address, the clouds parted and sudden brilliant sunshine illumined his face. Mary, sitting back of him on the platform, heard him speak the immortal words which were to echo down the years: "With malice toward none; with charity for all; with firmness in the right, as God gives us to see the right, let us strive on to finish the work we are in; to bind up the nation's wounds; to care for him who shall have borne the battle, and for his widow, and his orphan — to do all which may achieve and cherish a just, and a lasting peace, among ourselves, and with all nations."

Mr. Lincoln as well as Mary was fighting physical illness at this time. He told a friend a few days before the Inauguration that he was far from well. "My feet and hands of late seem to be always cold, and I ought perhaps to be in bed. . . ." Mary, looking at his thin face, was chilled with a strange foreboding. She did a curious thing that showed both her terrible anxiety and the extent to which her irrationality had progressed. In early March she bought a thousand dollars' worth of mourning goods.

Again she urged a trip to give him a change. They would go to the headquarters of the Union Army once more, to City Point, Virginia, where General Grant was in command. Their son Robert was now a captain on General Grant's staff and this was a strong added inducement. Again they embarked on a steamboat, this time one called *River Queen*. It was clear now that the war was in its final stage, with Union victory very near.

It would have been better for Mary if she had not taken that trip. Like her husband, she was in a state where perhaps she should have been in bed and she was destined to meet another carriage mishap. At City Point the President was to review the army. He rode out to the reviewing stand on horseback at the head of an impressive procession, but Mary went with Mrs. Grant in a carriage. The road was very rough, and once when they were going rapidly over a high bump the jolt lifted Mary clear of the seat and knocked her head against the top of the vehicle. What that severe blow on the head did to her cannot now be determined.

When she arrived at the reviewing place, she learned that the young and handsome wife of one of the generals had ridden on horseback beside the President at the head of the procession. Many of the soldiers had taken her for Mr. Lincoln's wife. Mary, jealous and in pain, went into a case of hysterics before a number of the officers. These military men did not know she was a sick woman who was not responsible for what she was doing. It was a painful incident for Mr. Lincoln and for Mary when she came to her senses again.

She was ill in bed for several days afterwards and wept in an agony of remorse over what she had done. She had tried for four years to fill her position as First Lady with grace and had made a magnificent record. Now it all seemed wiped out in those moments in which her failing had overwhelmed her. Not once before in those years had she made an outburst in public. And this unhappy incident had hurt Mr. Lincoln, whom she loved better than her own life.

Something he said to her during the visit to City Point further chilled her spirit. While taking a drive along the James River they had come to an old country graveyard. It looked so lovely with its flowers and tender green leaves of springtime that they got out of the carriage to stroll together among the quiet graves. Mr. Lincoln, weary and feeling the sense of peace in such a resting place, said, "Mary, you are younger than I. You will survive me. When I am gone, lay my remains in some quiet place like this." Her heart sank but she was to remember.

She was deeply depressed when the *River Queen* finally steamed back to the wharf near Washington on a Sunday evening, April 9. Then her spirit received an uplift. As she and Mr. Lincoln drove back to the White House, they passed through streets that were bright with bonfires and filled with shouting, rejoicing people. The news had come that General Lee had surrendered the Southern army to General Grant that afternoon. The great dividing Civil War was over and the Union was saved.

Washington went wild with celebration. On Monday, Mary wrote a friend: ". . . the crowds around the house have been immense, in the midst of the bands playing, they break forth into singing." On Tuesday evening the whole city was illuminated and thousands of feet were hurrying toward the White House to hear the President speak. He told them he wished to receive the Southerners back into the Union without bitterness or thought of revenge. On the day before, when a crowd had assembled, he had asked the surprised band to play "Dixie." It was as if he were saying to the conquered South, "Your song is now our song."

Mr. Lincoln's sleep of late had been broken by strange dreams. He told Mary and a close friend about one which haunted him. In his dream, he said, "There seemed to be a death-like stillness about me. Then I heard subdued sobs, as if a number of people were weeping. I thought I left my bed and wandered downstairs." He went from room to room, seeing no one but still the sobbing sound continued. Finally he entered the East Room. A body with covered face lay there in state with guards all around it. A great throng of people were assembled in the room and they were the ones who were "weeping pitifully." In his dream Mr. Lincoln asked one of the guards, "Who is dead in the White House?" "The President," answered the guard, "he was killed by an assassin!" Then came a fresh burst of grief from the crowd and Mr. Lincoln awoke, to sleep no more that night.

Mary was in terror at this recital. "That is horrid!" she cried. "I wish you had not told it." Then she tried to reassure herself and him by saying, "I am glad I don't believe in dreams. . . ." But she too was darkly haunted by this one.

On the Thursday night after General Lee's surrender, Mr. Lincoln had another dream, this time about a strange, mystic ship. He had had this same dream before, and always just prior to some momentous event such as a Union victory in battle. He told the members of his cabinet about it on Friday morning. In this dream he said, "that he seemed to be in some singular, indescribable vessel, and that he was moving with great rapidity towards an indefinite shore. . . ."

He was extremely happy that Friday, April 14. With Union victory and the ending of bloodshed, a great peace had come to him. His worn face was now almost radiant. Mary's heart was lifted with thankfulness too, especially as their son Robert came home from camp that morning. This seemed to put the seal on the fact that the war was over.

She and Mr. Lincoln were going for their usual drive that afternoon. She asked him whether she should invite anyone to go with them and he said, "No, I prefer to ride by ourselves to day." It was a day of days and he wanted to share with her his joy that his "great task" was finished, just as he had shared every good event with her through all the years they had been together. During the ride he was almost boyish in his gaiety and Mary, even while she was laughing at his playful remarks, said, "Dear Husband, you almost startle me, by your great cheerfulness." "And well I may feel so, Mary," he answered, "I consider *this day*, the war has come to a close." Then he added, "We must *both*, be more cheerful in the future — between the war & the loss of our darling Willie — we have both, been very miserable." So they talked of what they would do in that future, now that they could look forward to days and years that would be sweet and normal again. After all they had been through together they felt more close in companionship than ever.

They were planning to go to Ford's Theater that evening. When the hour approached, however, Mr. Lincoln was tired and Mary's head was aching, and they had half a mind to give up the idea. But then Mr. Lincoln said if they stayed at home he would have no rest, as he would have to talk to company all evening, and Mary thought they ought not to disappoint the people who expected to see them. They decided to go after all and with their two guests, Miss Clara Harris and her fiancé, they drove to the theater and entered it about eight-thirty.

All was pleasant and festive. Their box was decorated with flags, the play was a comedy, and the audience was exhilarated over the great victory and the coming of peace. Mary sat next to her husband, both gazing down at the brightly lighted stage. During the third act she found she had nestled close to Mr. Lincoln and had slipped her hand in his. It was an instinctive expression of that feeling of closeness they had, but, wondering how it would look to others, she said to him softly, "What will Miss Harris think of my hanging on to you so [?]" "She won't think anything about it," he replied, giving her an affectionate smile.

They were his last words to her. At that moment the assassin, John Wilkes Booth, was creeping up in the shadows behind them. A shot rang out and Mr. Lincoln slumped in his chair, unconscious.

What followed was a confused horror to Mary, beside herself with shock and grief. Doctors entered the box, men lifted the dying President and carried him to a house across the street from the theater. There he was laid on a bed in a small back room. In the crowding and wild confusion she did not know where he had been taken and kept crying out, "Where is my husband? Where is my husband?" until someone guided her to his bedside. Bending over him, she covered his unconscious face with kisses while she called to him with every endearing name and begged him to speak to her. He had never failed to respond to her tenderness before and she could not accept it that he was unable to do so now. She became convulsive in her grief and was led away into a front room.

All night long in that crowded little chamber Mr. Lincoln lay dying. Robert soon arrived and tried to do what he could for his mother. At intervals she would go back to her husband's bedside, to call to him again with the tender, loving names they had used in their happy years together. As the hours dragged on, she realized there was no hope and then she began to beg him to take her with him. Once she remembered his strange dream of people weeping over a dead body in the White House and cried out shudderingly, "His dream was prophetic." In her agony that night she prayed that she too might die.

After what seemed like endless hours, the grayness of dawn outlined the windows. Outside, a heavy rain was falling. For the last time Mary bent over her husband, kissed his dear face, and sobbed her words of love. At twenty-two minutes after seven Mr. Lincoln breathed his last.

Through the rain and the sorrowful tolling of bells she was driven back to the White House. The doctor said she must go to bed at once and those in attendance started to take her to her usual room. But she drew back. "Not there! Oh not there," she said. Not there in the room that still seemed warm with his living breath and the sweet feeling of closeness between them. So they took her to a room she had not used before.

Two lives had crashed that day. The sick and broken widow had received a wound that was fatal, though it would be years before she could die. Mr. Lincoln's mystic ship was safe in harbor; it was Mary's ship that must sail on and on through mist, darkness, and storm.

18

How a Great Wrong
Was Started

MRS. Lincoln still remains at the White House, more dead than alive, shattered and broken by the horrors of that dreadful night," wrote a sympathetic friend more than three weeks after Mr. Lincoln's death. It was necessary for her to leave the house as soon as possible but she was too ill to move. As after Willie's death, she alternated between strange spasms of grief and periods of complete prostration.

She did attend to one matter. In Illinois some citizens of Springfield, without consulting her, bought a section of land in the heart of the town for the President's burial place. When Mary learned this she remembered her husband's wish, as they had walked in the peaceful graveyard in Virginia, to rest "in some quiet place like this." She refused the town location and on May 4 he was buried in beautiful, quiet Oak Ridge Cemetery at Springfield. From that time on her supreme wish, as she repeatedly said, was to be buried "by the side of my darling husband."

I Mary

It was finally decided that she with her sons Robert and Tad should go to Chicago to live. On May 22 the frail, black-clad little woman walked for the last time down the White House stairs which she had so often radiantly descended on the arm of Mr. Lincoln. The three took inexpensive lodgings in Chicago, where Robert continued his study of law and Tad was placed in school. The pattern of Mary's life as a widow had begun.

According to the custom of the time a woman who had lost her husband must dress in plain black and live in seclusion without going to any kind of gathering or having any recreation. She must stay at home to weep and grieve. It was a very unwholesome plan for mental health but it was considered the proper thing to do and it was exactly what Mary in her sorrow wanted to do.

Living in boardinghouses, staying in her room, and having no activities, she spent much of her time writing letters, letters often on black-bordered paper, for even her stationery must indicate that she was in deep mourning. Reading these many letters, you can look directly into her mind and learn all her anguished thoughts in those dark days.

Love, grief, and reverence for her dead husband make up the most part of those letters. She could hardly accept it that he was gone. "I, sometimes," she wrote, "in my wildness and grief, am tempted to believe that it is some *terrible, terrible* dream, and that my idolized husband will return to me." Repeatedly she spoke of her feeling that he was "only 'Gone before' and I am certain is fondly watching and waiting for our re-union, nevermore to be separated." Then she would say, "I must patiently await, the hour, when, 'God's love,' shall place me, by *his* side again."

Now that Mr. Lincoln's protecting devotion had been taken away, she realized that he had spoiled her and the children by his indulgence. There is self-reproach in her letters for the times her quick tongue had hurt him. "I doubtless trespassed, many times & oft, upon his great tenderness & amiability of character," she wrote once and in another letter she expressed the passionate wish that "I could have asked forgiveness, for any inadvertent moment of pain, I may have caused him."

One thing in which she found comfort was the memory of the great, single devotion he had given her through the years. She wrote a friend shortly after Mr. Lincoln's death, "It was always, music in my ears, both before & after our marriage, when my husband, told me, that I was the only one, he had ever thought of or cared for." She had given him a great love and had received a great love from him in return. That had been the glory of her life and nothing could take that away from her.

Or so it seemed. But even as she wrote those words, Fate was preparing to strike at this one sustaining comfort she had left. That maladjusted individual in Springfield, William Herndon, was about to assume his role of villain in Mary's life drama.

I Mary

To understand what happened, it is necessary to know certain things about Herndon. Matters had not gone too well with him after Mr. Lincoln left Springfield. His law practice had dwindled and it was hard for him to get along. People are not inclined to give their law business to a man they see drunk and irresponsible on the streets. Many also considered him "a crank" because of the queer ideas he was always talking about.

His weakness for allowing his mind to be "improperly directed," as Mr. Lincoln had put it, had greatly increased. He had reached the point where he actually believed he could read people's minds and tell what they were thinking. He also had a fixed idea that he always knew what was the truth by his own instinct or intuition. A man who is convinced of these two notions ends by believing just what he wants to believe. Herndon was to tell many cruel falsehoods about Mary and Mr. Lincoln but he believed them at the moment he said them. This saves him from being considered a deliberate liar but points up the fact that he was an ill-balanced, flighty person whose statements were often based on his own imagination and could not be trusted.

After Mr. Lincoln's death people began to study and write about him. Some came to Springfield and they naturally questioned Herndon, who had been his law partner for many years. Herndon found this new attention very stimulating. He had never been considered so important before. Very soon he decided that he too would write about Mr. Lincoln. He set out to collect all the information he could about the great President for the purpose of writing a book about his life.

One day in the summer of 1866 Robert Lincoln in Chicago told his mother he had a letter from William Herndon. This letter said Herndon would like to talk with Mrs. Lincoln to ask her some questions about Mr. Lincoln and herself. The one subject Mary always wanted to talk about was Mr. Lincoln and she believed Herndon, with all his faults, had been devoted to him. (She did not know the disappointed and frustrated Herndon was nursing a great hatred against her.) She answered the letter herself, agreeing to see him and writing graciously (with her usual excess of commas): ". . . the knowledge, of your great love & reverence, for the best man, that ever lived, would of *itself*, cause you, to be cherished, with the sincerest regard, by my sons & myself." She was planning to go to Springfield to visit the tomb "which contains my All, in life" and she would see him at her hotel at that time.

When they met Herndon had been drinking and Mary said afterwards she was revolted at the smell of liquor on his breath. He began asking her questions and writing down her answers and this record can be read today. Mary gave a wonderful and understanding description of Mr. Lincoln and fairly poured out her heart in telling how he had been the "most loving husband and father in the world."

Her words fell on deaf ears. Herndon did not let proven facts stand in the way of his believing what he wanted to believe. Two months later, to Mary living in sad seclusion in Chicago (her one comfort the memory of her husband's devotion and her belief that he was fondly waiting for her on the other side), came the news that Herndon in a public lecture in Springfield had said that Mr. Lincoln had never loved his wife at all. Herndon stated that Mr. Lincoln, when a young man living in New Salem, had loved a Miss Ann Rutledge, that they became engaged, and when she died his heart was buried in her grave. Herndon went on to proclaim that Lincoln had never loved any other woman, saying to prove this that he never signed his letters to any woman "yours affectionately." The utter falseness of the last is shown by Mr. Lincoln's loving letters to Mary, which can be read today and which are signed either "Affectionately" or "Most affectionately."

Mary in her indignation and horror thought that Herndon's mind was affected, as well she might. She had never heard the name Ann Rutledge. Mr. Lincoln had lived in New Salem before she ever met him, and while she was willing to admit that most people might have "a little romance in their early days," she had a good reason for knowing that Mr. Lincoln had never given his heart to any other woman except herself, ". . . as my husband was *truth itself*, and as he always assured me, he had cared for no one but myself. . . ." She did not believe a word of Herndon's story. Remembering all the joy and devotion she had shared with Mr. Lincoln through the years, she continued, "Nor did his

life or his joyous laugh, lead one to suppose his heart,
was in any unfortunate woman's grave — but in the
proper place with his loved wife & children."

The question at once arises, how did Herndon get the
idea for this lecture? While collecting material about his
senior partner's early life, he learned that Mr. Lincoln
had known a girl named Ann Rutledge at New Salem.
He had boarded for a while at her father's house, the
Rutledge tavern, and Ann had undoubtedly helped to
cook his meals. She was engaged to be married to John
McNamar, a friend of Mr. Lincoln's whom he called
Mack. While Mack was off on a long trip and out of
touch with New Salem, Ann became ill and died. Mr.
Lincoln was deeply grieved, as were all the people in
the little settlement. The death of this sweet young
woman with her lover far away was a pitiful and tragic
thing. One of Mr. Lincoln's friends, seeing how badly
he felt over Ann's death, wondered idly whether he had
been in love with her. It was a mere passing conjecture.
John McNamar, Ann's lover, returned from his trip
expecting to marry her, and he was the one who went
sadly to her grave and carved her initials on the head-
board.

These are the facts upon which Herndon built up the
irresponsible statements in his lecture. There is not a
scrap of reliable evidence that Lincoln was in love with
Ann. But it was to be more than a century after Ann's
death before historians could get at the records and
bring Herndon, as it were, before the court of historical

justice. Historians now know that the supposed Lincoln-Rutledge romance is a misty folktale and not real history.

Herndon wanted passionately to believe that Lincoln had loved Ann. Convinced as he was that he knew what was true by his own superior power of intuition, he did believe it. The story served his purpose doubly; it made an appealing, poetic tale to put into his book on Lincoln and it caused bitter anguish to Mary Lincoln, whom he hated.

Herndon was to spend many years assembling material for his book and then theorizing over it. In the end this man with his imaginings, obsessions, and corroding hatred used the supposed Rutledge romance to erase one of the grandest things in Lincoln's life, his complete devotion to Mary, the only woman, as he himself said, that he had ever loved. What Herndon did was to take away from the American public one of the finest love stories in its history and put in its place a flimsy legend.

An unsound incident inserted into the story of a life acts like a rotten apple in a barrel of good apples: it destroys the soundness of the others around it. Herndon had to destroy Lincoln's true romance with Mary Todd in order to build up his theory that Lincoln had never loved anyone but Ann. It is interesting to see the way he went about this. He took the incident of the broken engagement between Mary and Mr. Lincoln and turned it into a wedding occasion at which Lincoln as bridegroom failed to appear. Out of his imagination Herndon described in his book a wedding scene that never existed: "The bride, bedecked in veil and silken gown, and nervously toying with the flowers in her hair," the assembled guests, the anxious waiting for the groom to come, and the terrible dismay and humiliation for Mary when he did not appear. (This was making Mr. Lincoln act like a cad.) It is a vivid description, however, for Herndon could use colorful language and as he once said, when he "wished to say something smart," he would sometimes take "a Toddy as *Exciter*."

Herndon could not get around the fact that Mr. Lincoln married Mary. It would ruin his theory that Lincoln never loved any woman except Ann to admit that he married Mary because he loved her. So Herndon had to invent a theory to explain their marriage. He said Mr. Lincoln did not love Mary but he "married Mary Todd to save his honor," because he had promised to marry her. As a minister friend of the Lincolns pointed out at the time of Herndon's lecture, it made Lincoln "worse than a dishonest man" if he had promised "to love and to cherish" for all his life a woman he did not love.

Herndon further said that Mary was so humiliated by Lincoln's deserting her at the altar (which never happened) that she never loved him again and he suggested that she married him for revenge! "Love fled at the approach of revenge," says his book.

Such were Herndon's made-up incidents and ridiculous theories which blotted out the love and devoted marriage of Mary and her husband and falsified the characters of both. Of course with this start Herndon pictured the marriage as a very unhappy one and Mary as a cold, disagreeable, heartless shrew who made her husband miserable. As Herndon's fortunes sank lower and lower, his bitterness and hatred toward Mary increased until there was nothing too terrible for him to say about her.

Herndon's *Life of Lincoln* was finally published in his old age. He did not have what it takes to write a book — in the end he had to get another man to put his rambling materials (letters, notes, and the like) into some sort of order, straighten out some of his contradictions, and put the whole into presentable English. There is much in the book which is valuable, but where it touches upon Lincoln's love, his marriage, and Mary his wife, it is a case of Herndon riding his theories.

The public, however, for a long time accepted Herndon's conclusions. People reasoned that he had been Lincoln's law partner and therefore ought to know what he was talking about. Other writers on Lincoln repeated the Ann Rutledge legend and the whole bill of goods that went with it, that Mary was an awful woman and the marriage was terribly unhappy. So the flimsy legend and the slander about Mary were embedded in books, articles, poems and plays which still have a wide audience. This is why today you can read books, otherwise excellent, which repeat the Ann Rutledge myth and defame Mary Lincoln.

It takes a long time for truth crushed to earth to rise

again. Through many years historians, quietly searching old letters, diaries and papers, were unearthing evidence (such as the loving letters between Lincoln and his wife) which showed how wrong Herndon was in saying their marriage had been loveless and unhappy. It was not until the 1940s, however, that Herndon's own collection of papers was opened to the public. These papers contained his so-called "evidence" about the supposed Lincoln-Rutledge romance and at last it was possible to show how untrustworthy it was. After these papers were opened, Herndon himself was thoroughly studied by a careful historian and his weaknesses (such as his obsession that he knew what was true by intuition) were fully revealed.

Americans have a fine sense of what is fair and just. It is painful to realize the injustice that was so long done to Mary and the cruelty of the things that were said about her. This feeling is beautifully expressed in a poem by Jane Merchant which appeared in the Washington *Star* on February 14, 1955. The very fact that such a poem has been written is a heartwarming sign that at last justice to Mary is being done.

VALENTINE FOR MARY LINCOLN

Forgive us, Mary, for the cruel lies
   We long believed of you; that you were only
A nagging burden to the patient, wise,
   Great-hearted man who bore the anguished, lonely

I Mary

Weight of a warring nation. We have thought
    You gave him little help or tenderness
And with self-centered, angry tempers brought
    More sorrow to him in his great distress.
We have grown wiser now; we know you gave
    Him love and understanding without measure,
And were warm-hearted, kind, and deeply brave —
    I write you this to tell you that we treasure
Your memory; and most of all, to tell
You that we know, at last, he loved you well.

19

"I Will Be Comforted"

*M*ARY, living in Chicago not far from Springfield, burned with humiliation after Herndon's lecture on Ann Rutledge. She did not accept the supposed love affair, but to have people all over the country believing that she and Mr. Lincoln had never loved each other was a falsehood and an injustice to them both that was well nigh unbearable. She could do nothing to stop Herndon from proclaiming his theories and the frustration of this was hard to take. She probably felt at the end of that year of 1866 that Fate had done its worst, but other strange, tragic experiences were ahead for her.

The letters she was writing around this time were full of two subjects. The first was the goodness and greatness of the husband for whom she was mourning. The second was her terrible worry over her poverty and debts. After the assassination of Mr. Lincoln the bills for all those luxurious clothes she had bought began to pile in upon her.

Her husband's death had made her sense of insecurity

complete. Her belief that she was in dreadful poverty was now unshakable. It was true that her means had been greatly reduced and she could not afford to have a fine house and run it with the dignity which she felt was required of a President's widow. Mr. Lincoln, however, had left an estate which furnished money enough for her to live in a quiet manner.

Those bills were a frightful complication. She was honest and of course she must pay her debts. But how? She tried pawning a few of her belongings at a little pawnshop in Chicago, but that was hardly a drop in the bucket. At times Mary would even go without her dinner to save a few pennies.

She decided she must sell all the expensive dresses, furs, and jewels that had caused the trouble. She would not need or wear them now, as she always dressed in plain black and never went to any parties or entertainments.

Dreading public notice, she wanted no one to know she was selling her clothes. She traveled to New York, where, heavily veiled and using the assumed name of Mrs. Clarke, she visited the firm of W. H. Brady on Broadway to arrange the sale. Of course the people at the Brady firm soon found out they were dealing with Mrs. Abraham Lincoln and they set out to get all the publicity they could for themselves. When she realized that they knew who she was, she suggested they try to sell some of the articles to prominent politicians whom she had known while in the White House. The Brady people, telling her they would make a great deal of money for her, persuaded her to write them some letters; then they published these letters and mentioned certain prominent politicians. This caused a blaze of newspaper publicity and threw the whole affair into the boiling pot of politics.

Mary, longing only to be left unnoticed in her seclusion and grief, once more found herself the target of public gossip and misrepresentation. The slanders, as they passed from tongue to tongue, increased like a rolling snowball. The terrible stories that had been circulated when she was in the White House were revived and aired, even the accusation she had been a Confederate spy.

People were so inflamed over the various tales that she was afraid to appear on the streets. "I suppose I would be *mobbed* if I ventured out," she wrote at this time, saying in another letter that she could not be more defamed "If I had committed murder in every city in this *blessed Union*."

She did not make money out of the unfortunate venture and she could not even get her clothes back from the Brady firm until the following year. Mary did in the end, however, pay her debts. It took time and sacrifice, but finally she was able to write a friend that every bill was paid, adding, "I can assure you — in perfect truth that *many dinnerless* days, have fallen to *my* portion in consequence of *all this*." This letter was stained with her tears.

Dreading to venture in public and with newspapers still printing accusations about her, Mary in 1868 decided to take Tad and go to Europe for a while. To escape "persecution from the vampyre press," she wrote, "I had to flee to a land of strangers for refuge." She felt she could leave Robert, who had become a lawyer and had married that fall, so that he now had a home of his own.

So it came about one day in October of that year a little woman dressed in mourning, with a fifteen-year-old son, was seen going on board a ship bound for foreign parts. Long before, when she was a bright-faced, happy wife, she had expressed her longing to cross the ocean on one of the big steamers, but that wish had included going with Mr. Lincoln. It seemed a cruel irony that she was fleeing from the country which he had saved.

Her plan was to go to Frankfurt on the Main in Germany and place Tad in a good school there. She would get a room where she could see him often and they would travel around together during his vacations. This was to be the pattern of their lives for nearly three years abroad, and in those years Tad became the center of Mary's life, her one reason for existence.

She always had to have someone on whom to pour out the wealth of her deep affection. She loved Robert, who was a good and conscientious son, but he was not like his father. Taddie, however, had grown more and more like Mr. Lincoln in his understanding and love.

In those dreadful days after the assassination three

years before, Tad had been the only one who could help her. When he would hear her sobbing in the night he would get up, go to her bedside, and whisper wise little words of comfort. "Don't cry, Mamma; I cannot sleep if you cry! Papa was good, and he has gone to heaven. He is happy there. He is with God and my brother Willie. Don't cry, Mamma, or I will cry too." Mary would hold him close in her arms and try to calm herself for his sake.

As he grew taller during those years in Germany, it was evident he had inherited the slender build of his father and there was an unmistakable resemblance in his face. Mary, living in cheap, uncomfortable lodgings, existed only for the hours she spent with him. She was often ill and then the boy would leave his school to nurse her. "Taddie," she wrote once, "is like some *old woman*, with regard to his care of me — and two or three days since — when I was *so very* sick — his dark loving eyes — watching over me, reminded me so much of his dearly beloved father's — so filled with *his* deep love."

During Tad's summer vacation in 1869 the two visited Mary's former pastor in Springfield, who was now living in Scotland. Her letters about this trip show much of her old interest and enthusiasm. She delighted in the beautiful scenes of lakes and mountains and in visiting the birthplace of Robert Burns, whose poems Mr. Lincoln had loved. And it was so good to be with the old friend who could talk of the happy Springfield days.

Autumn brought the welcome news from across the

water that a child had been born to Robert and his wife. At last Mary had a little girl of her own blood to love, a granddaughter named Mary Lincoln for her. She poured out her affection and longing in a letter to Robert's wife: "That blessed baby, how dearly I would love to look upon her sweet young face." She hoped the little family would come to Germany to see her and Tad. "I do so trust that Bob will come over with you if it is only for three months . . . He loves you so *very dearly* . . . You know you will always be *First Love* of daughters-in-law."

In the summer of 1870 the Congress in Washington voted a pension for the widow of President Lincoln. This was news Mary had long hoped for and she could afford to live more comfortably with this pension added to what she had. Her obsession that she was very poor, however remained fixed irrationally in her mind.

That summer she and Tad went to Austria for his vacation and were caught in the outbreak of the Franco-Prussian War. Mary knew only too well what war meant and making their escape was a nerve-racking experience for her. "My heart has been made sick the past summer, by being *almost* in the midst of the fearful war, which has convulsed the Continent," she wrote a friend that fall from England, to which she and Tad had fled.

They were weary now of travel and were homesick to see Robert and his little family, who had not been able to cross the ocean to see them. By the spring of 1871 the two exiles had decided to come home. After a stormy voyage they finally reached Chicago in May. At last Mary had the joy of holding her little granddaughter in her arms, and perhaps now she felt she could live in Chicago with some measure of peace. It was, however, all too brief a period of rejoicing she had, for Fate was preparing for her two final, terrible tragedies.

Tad became sick with a severe cold soon after they arrived. He improved at first, then had a relapse. Early in June, Mary wrote a friend, "My dear boy has been *very, very* dangerously ill. . . . I have been sitting up . . . constantly for the last ten nights. . . ." Six weeks of intense anxiety and suffering went by with alternate hope and despair, then on July 15 Tad's dear loving eyes were closed forever.

He was the last person who needed Mary and the great love she had to give. Robert had his wife and baby and he had never been as understanding and close to his mother as Willie and Tad. Mary said in her complete desolation, "I feel that there is no life to me, without my idolized Taddie."

She traveled around in this country trying to get away from the sadness which she carried in her own heart. Two years passed after Tad's death, and then in December, 1873, Herndon gave another lecture in Springfield. Herndon by this time, like Mary herself, had become an object to stir deep pity. Hard times and his own qualities had reduced him to extreme poverty. Living on a farm six miles out of Springfield, he made a pathetic picture when he walked into town, so down at the heel and unkempt that little boys were told there was a bird's nest in his shaggy beard. Yet he was still a man filled with hate and a deadly power to injure.

Herndon prided himself on not believing in Christianity and churchgoing, and in this lecture he proclaimed that Mr. Lincoln had not believed in them either. Mary's husband had attended church with her, and few have lived the Christian ideals and put their trust in God as completely as Abraham Lincoln. But Herndon said in his lecture that he had not been a Christian. Mary, whose deep religious faith was her one comfort, was in agony over this gross injustice to her husband.

By this time Herndon's theories and fabrications were being talked of over the whole country: The Ann Rutledge legend with its corollary that Mr. Lincoln had never loved his wife, the made-up tale about his failing to show up at his own wedding, and the accusation that he had not been a Christian. Mary and her son Robert tried to get Herndon to desist from saying these things but that only made him proclaim them more loudly. Mary was in despair. "What more can I say," she wrote, "in answer to this man, who when my heart was broken with anguish, issued falsehoods, against me & mine, which were enough to make the Heavens blush."

There is a limit to what one person can take. Perhaps it is to be wondered at that Mary, emotionally unstable as she was, had endured the tragedies of her life as well as she had. Now she began having delusions of persecution, imagining that people were trying to injure her or kill her. Her existence became a nightmare of fear. At night, sleepless, she would walk the floor with the lights turned high, eying her windows with dread of the nameless terror that might come through them. If food tasted strange to her, she thought someone was trying to poison her. When she entered a public dining room she would whisper, "I am afraid; I am afraid."

Robert, her last remaining son, tried to do everything he could to help and protect her. He wanted to take her into his own home but she would not agree to that. She traveled around carrying many thousands of dollars in her undergarments and he was in terror that she would be robbed and murdered. Her mania for buying was causing her again to spend large sums of money. The only possible way he could get control of her money (to save it for her) and put her under the medical care which she needed was to have her adjudged insane by a court of law. Robert, with a heavy heart, arranged a sanity hearing for his mother.

Few scenes have been more heartbreaking than the one in the courtroom in Chicago on May 19, 1875. Mary, on trial for insanity, sat quietly and intelligently listening as Robert and various doctors on the witness stand told of her hysterical behavior and imaginings. A pitying newspaperman described her as "gentle looking and modestly attired." Robert in his testimony told how good she had always been to him and several times he broke down and wept. It was Mary's last public appearance and never had she borne herself with more dignity and composure.

The jury returned a verdict of insanity. Robert then, with pale, tearstained face, went to his mother and tenderly took her hand. She said to him in stunned unbelief, "O Robert, to think that my son would ever have done this." For Mary, who of course did not realize that she was irrational in any way whatever, believed that Robert had planned this trial in order to steal her money. This seemed the ultimate in tragedy — that she thought the son she loved had betrayed her.

She was taken to a private sanitarium where everything was made as pleasant and easy for her as possible. The care and protection she received did have the effect of calming her hysterical fears and she appeared entirely normal to friends who visited her. Robert had said truly that his mother was "sane on all subjects but one." If those with her did not touch on her supposed poverty and her extravagance, they saw no sign of irrationality about her.

After less than four months in the sanitarium she convinced influential friends that she had been wrongfully put there. Through their efforts she was allowed to go to the Edwards home in Springfield where she had lived when Mr. Lincoln first courted her. Her sister Elizabeth had opposed their marriage because she thought it was her family duty, but with that same family loyalty Elizabeth now welcomed Mary and took care of her.

Nine months later a second court trial pronounced her sane again.

Blaming Robert bitterly for having the sanity trial, Mary would have nothing to do with him. Proud and sensitive, she felt she could not stay in a country that believed she was insane. "I cannot endure to meet my former friends, Lizzie," she said to Mrs. Edwards, "they will never cease to regard me as a lunatic, I feel it in their soothing manner. If I should say the moon is made of green cheese they would heartily and smilingly agree with me. I love you, but I cannot stay. I would be much less unhappy in the midst of strangers."

Once more she fled abroad into what she herself called "an *exile*." For the next four years she made her headquarters at Pau, France, though she visited various other cities. Speaking only French, she again had reason to remember Madame Mentelle's training with gratitude. Her health was failing rapidly now and she was often ill. The only thing she longed for was the time when she could join her husband and children on the other side. The waiting seemed so long to her.

One day in her lodgings while trying to hang a picture over the mantel, she fell from the stepladder, receiving a painful, lasting injury to her spine. Her weight was scarcely a hundred pounds now and she realized she must go back to her own people. In the fall of 1880 she wrote the Edwards family in Springfield, "I cannot trust myself, *any longer* away from you all — I am too ill & feeble in health."

Again the faithful sister Lizzie received her back into her home. There Robert came trying to make peace with his mother. He brought with him his little daughter, Mary Lincoln, and his mother's affectionate heart could not hold out against her son and grandchild. She promised to forgive and forget.

In her final illness the shadows in her brain deepened. She seemed closer to those who had "gone before." Once after a severe illness abroad she had written, "I have been so near my husband — there were days of delirium — when I can quite recall — that my dearly loved ones — were hanging over me. . . ." Now her wifely devotion was outlasting her worn-out body and clouded mind: she told one who was ministering to her that the place on the bed beside her was the President's place. Her love for him was greater than her life.

Mary died at the Edwards home on July 16, 1882. The news was telegraphed over the country and came to the ears of that stanch little woman Jane Swisshelm, who had met her at the White House reception long before and loved her ever since. Jane found it "sad, glad tidings," because she remembered what Mrs. Lincoln had said to her, "Ah, my dear friend, you will rejoice when you know that I have gone to my husband and children."

The funeral was stately and beautiful as Mary herself would have wished it. Among the many banked-up tributes of flowers was one in the form of a large book made of carnations with the name *Mary Lincoln* in blue forget-me-nots on the opened pages. It came as "the loving offering of the people" of Springfield, those who were remembering the friendly, joyous girl and the kind, affectionate neighbor she had been.

A great crowd of friends stood by in the cemetery when she was laid in the place she had longed to be, beside her husband. "When I again rest by *his* side, I will be comforted," she had said. "And the *waiting*, is so long."

The cruel years were over. Mary was at last united with her Mr. Lincoln and was at peace.

Index

Index

Lincoln, Abraham (*continued*)

    hours, death, 205–208; and Ann Rutledge, in Herndon's story, 214–219; and religion, in Herndon's story, 227–228

Lincoln, Edward Baker, son of Mary, birth and childhood, 85–86, 93, 94, 98–100; illness and death, 104–106, 170

Lincoln, Mary, granddaughter of Mary, 226, 227, 232

Lincoln, Mary Todd (Mrs. Abraham Lincoln), childhood appearance, personality, experiences, 3–35 *passim;* love of clothes, finery, 3–9, 40–41, 117, 121–122, 138–139, 150–151, 152–155, 200, 222; sensitiveness to criticism, 6, 12, 159, 193; family background and environment, 10–35 *passim;* personal relations with Negroes, 11–34, 94, 152–155, 158, 174, 180–181, 185, 199; education, 13–14, 17–32; social grace (animation, poise, friendliness), 18–20, 21, 28–32 *passim,* 40–47, 114, 116–122 *passim,* 146, 150–159 *passim,* 165–166, 170–172, 181–184; and Henry Clay, 20–21, 25, 50–51, 89; attitude toward slavery, 24–26, 158, 180–181, 185; and Emilie Helm, 31, 88, 93–94, 116–122, 129, 162, 190–195

Residence with Edwardses (1839–1842), 33–34, 36–74 *passim;* love of travel, 36, 130, 133–134, 224; democratic attitude, 44–45, 59, 137–138, 156; Lincoln's courtship of, 46–73; shared Lincoln's interests, 47–55, 75, 127, 131–133, 205–206; courted by Douglas, 48, 58, 59–60; courted by Webb, 49, 53–55, 61–62; love of all children, 49, 76, 108–110, 169–173; shared Lincoln's political ambitions and interests, 50–51, 86–87, 114, 127, 130–136, 196, 200; youthful ideal of marriage, 52–53, 59; and Todd family opposition to her marriage, 53–73, 79; terms of address used between Lincoln and, 56, 77, 143–144, 167

Wedding plans and ceremony, 64–73; and "Rebecca" letters affair, 65–67; housekeeper and homemaker, 74–87, 101–143 *passim;* confidence in Lincoln's destiny, 75, 86–87, 96, 127, 131–132, 150, 200–201; burden of Lincoln's absences on circuit, 76, 103, 113–114; birth of her children, 76–77, 85–86, 107–110; and Robert Lincoln, 77–79, 134, 186, 207, 210, 224, 226–232; child-rearing methods and devotion to her chil-

Index